The Joys of
Childminding

ISBN 978-1-7394533-0-5 (paperback)

ISBN 978-1-7394533-1-2 (ebook)

Book design by Leanne Booth

Various images by Freepik

Acknowledgements

To be successful in doing what you love is a great achievement, but to be surrounded by people who constantly remind you this, is a blessing.

Firstly, thank you to my husband and my 'besties' who love me unconditionally; giving me endless support throughout the compilation of this book.

To Mum and Dad, for supporting my career choices throughout life. I appreciate all the trips to the library every Sunday that nurtured my love of learning and enthusiasm for physical activities.

To Julian Grenier, for your inspirational, empowering qualities, and for always wearing a smile and having something positive to say. And to Tracey Warden, for being a friend, a guide and someone to turn to.

To Matemi, for believing in me since day one.

Childminding would not be the same without our beautiful community; everyone who brightens up our day by simply saying 'hello,' giving us such wonderful praise and going to great efforts to interact with us. Thank you!

But most of all, this book is dedicated to my childminding beauties who serenade me with love and accept me as I am. I have the best job in the world in preparing you for the dreams you will one day make realities.

Contents

Introduction

I began childminding after years of working within numerous childcare settings including nurseries, pre-schools and home-based au pair work. During my time as a childcare assistant, I learnt the dos and don'ts first hand, which helped me to visualise an outstanding setting for looked-after children. I also realised that I was not happy to work under management; I felt I could not work to the best of my ability or use my initiative efficiently. Therefore, I made sure my childminding courses were completed whilst doing some more nannying, and finally started my own childminding business thereafter. Business was very slow to begin with, but I am glad I had that time to pace myself. Quality was always on my agenda, as opposed to quantity, aka quickly expanding my business to a bigger scale, as I was advised by family members. Luckily for me I was smart enough to know that they were not taking into account all my goals, but looking solely at an opportunity for me to profit, or at the very least, make money. Since then, there have been quiet and difficult times as well as very busy periods that have pushed me to make some big changes.

Even though my job has been difficult at times and began with slow financial progress, the positive aspects have kept me going through the darkest times in my life; the families' continuous support and praise, along with the children's warmth, have given me the motivation I needed to persist.

People always advise that I should keep personal and work aspects of life separate; however, a blurring of the two can easily happen when assistants, parents and carers are mixing daily. I have learnt how to manage boundaries which helps the business run smoothly. One of these is that personal/ private matters should not be discussed in the setting. If I was not happy with my job role, I would not be able to operate with as much enthusiasm and energy as I do, therefore it is important to consider how much you love (or

don't love) the way in which childminding blends into your life.

Childminding requires team work even though it can also be isolating at times. Having said this, there are always people you can reach out to for support. However, being cautious not to let others take advantage and take credit is necessary to ensure your hard work is properly rewarded. You can do it, just as I did, and all you need is smart thinking as well as the confidence to take sole responsibility for your business. Whether operating on a larger scale with many staff members or working alone, the same rules apply; getting to know children on a one-to-one basis is important, so my advice is to start small then progress.

I have written this book to give others an insight into childminding as a profession, and I have written it with a positive mindset because there is so much joy to be discovered. I found that after the Covid-19 lockdown, there were so many childminders leaving their jobs and reaching out for support because they were struggling with certain aspects of the day to day. The childminding Facebook groups have been helpful in that I've felt I've been a part of a network group who have supported each other with care. I love to see their ideas, advice and photos of their settings, and I know that I can quickly post a message to ask a question. The responses have always been very positive. The height of the Covid-19 era seemed to cause a decline in everyone's mental health and financial stability. It was tough; however, I think we should be proud of ourselves and celebrate our achievements for making it through. This book is a celebration of our fight to keep our businesses going despite the hardships faced. I want to highlight the joys of childminding to shine a light on what we do and how fantastic a job it is, but also how courageous it is to take on the responsibilities of an early-years role.

How to begin

- **Find a learning centre** near you or an online learning platform that offers level 2 and 3 in childcare, business start-up and childminding courses.

- **Contact your local children's centre** and begin attending.

- **Join Facebook groups** or follow Instagram pages; here you can ask for advice and get ideas from others.

- **Watch YouTube videos** on how other childminders operate and run their settings.

- **Research childcare settings around you** and establish what you will offer. Remember your prices may be higher than others nearby.

- **Write up a business plan** and consider the first few years may be slow, so be realistic.

- **Register and advertise on free websites** first, then choose one to join for a fee if necessary.

- **Hand out leaflets during school pick-ups**, drop-offs and trips.

- **Only decrease your fees if necessary** and do not feel obliged to give discounts.

- **Consider the Early Years Foundation Stage (EYFS)** and buy a diverse range of resources that link to each of the seven areas. Look out for heuristic play resources such as loose parts and make them with the children, for example sensory bottles or rainbow ribbon rings.

Stay composed and have faith

It's so easy to accidentally change our usual ways of working, melting under the pressure of being watched, whether it's by a new employee or Ofsted. It is an inspector's job to record what they see in detail, so there is (understandably) a lot of pressure to get everything 'right'. The key thing to remember is that you have years of training and knowledge to guide you, so, going with your gut instinct is most likely reliable. I have often questioned myself when I've been working with someone else, whether an assistant or a fellow childcare professional. For example, I would hesitate when they questioned my ways of working or change my usual routine spontaneously to something they wanted to see. A short while after, I would realise there's a reason for the procedures I have in place, and I can confidently explain this to the assistant. I think we all need to remind ourselves of the core aspects of our setting that help it run accordingly day to day.

Only you know the achievements you have gained over the years and how your setting is built around those. I understand how it may seem unfair to be judged within such a short timeframe, however, just doing what you already do every day and being confident simultaneously is essential. Wendy Ratcliff, inspector at Ofsted for early-years education, advises just this; Ofsted want to know what it is like for a child attending the setting every day, and for us not to feel pressured by doing things differently. She also shares that children will notice straight away if something is different (Ratcliff 2023). This makes me feel reassured!

On receiving my first 'good' grade I was frustrated at the fact that I had worked so hard to try and be an 'outstanding' childminder, and still it was not good enough. I learnt two things from this situation: there is a fine line between the two grades and to know what is expected prior to the first inspection, is very difficult. To overcome this hurdle, The Education Inspection Framework (Ofsted, 2023) is a useful document to read; in that it highlights how Ofsted

inspect.

My second inspection was carried out by an incredibly friendly, chatty lady who seemed to want me to do well from the moment she entered my home. She was extremely positive and encouraging so I felt confident from the moment she walked in! By comparison, the first inspector was much stricter, marking me down for placing limits to the child's creativity during a water play activity I had set up. He said I hadn't let the child move around freely and choose her own toys, however she'd wanted to carry a cup of water around which I'd said no to and for good reason! The inspector had already made up his mind and the girl had refused to put the cup down, so that was the end of that. I do wonder if she had spilt water all over the floor, would I have been marked down for the hazard created? We may not always agree with the way we have been inspected; however, we should focus on what is within our control instead. If there are concerns over how an inspection has been carried out, there is an opportunity to appeal against a decision, but I always tell myself it's better to wait until my initial response has passed, then review the situation thoroughly before taking any action. Since these two inspections

(2016 and 2019), I can hand on heart say I now feel the quality of my childcare setting is much higher than before, which means I have progressed.

You will learn and grow from the first inspection which is a positive to take forward. Whichever grade we are awarded, if the parents and children are happy, we should be proud of what we are doing well, then start an action plan to work on the weaknesses. If you know you strive to go above and beyond for them, regardless of judgement from external sources, try to review your practise whilst not letting your self-esteem take the fall.

I have seen nursery staff running around changing the whole layout of a playroom when Ofsted arrive without warning; it has puzzled me to see, because surely a setting should not be in that bad of a state to begin with. Doing all of this whilst there are employees present does not model good practise, but it does teach them what not to do. One thing about changing the daily routine or layout is it will most likely change the children's usual behaviour. Try for as little change as possible, I say, for an inspection. Think about how much children familiarise themselves with a setting during the settling-in period; they become attached to particular resources and will go to them as soon as they arrive each day. Children know exactly where everything is and can be independent in accessing it, therefore they need that familiarity. It is similar to the way we adults get annoyed when we cannot find something we left in a certain spot (or think we did); I do it all the time! I like my things where I can find them and love a sense of familiarity.

It is a daily struggle for childminders to maintain a safe, clean and tidy playroom, not just at inspection time and especially if we cannot afford a cleaner, but there are ways to make the process easier. Many settings rotate resources or close for an inset day to clean. I tend to inspect my playroom as if I were a third party, taking down old or ripped displays, for example.

Advice and ideas:

· Prioritise the actions needed rather than trying to perfect everything; list a few actions and get them done before your inspection.

· Do a bit at a time (paperwork/cleaning/sanitising), so you're not overexerting yourself.

· Ask yourself if children know where everything is, if they can reach what they want and be independent in setting up/tidying up.

· Keep an evaluation book and note down things you notice that are working and things that aren't. Monitor the progress made and tick off the completed tasks, now feel a whole lot of satisfaction!

You're so patient

I can't count the number of times people have said to me, 'You must be so patient to work with children,' suggesting my levels of patience and tolerance are high, and that the child is learning through my teaching. If children are not encouraged to wait, they can become used to getting what they want, when they want it! For example, I use time-related language and the concept of waiting during toy washing machine or toy oven role play. You can also use this throughout the day, when you are baking or explaining the next routine to a child for example. 'In five minutes, it will be [Child A's] turn,' we might say. It is necessary to make them wait sometimes, even if it's just two minutes at a time. This is the only way to avoid the common 'I want it now' phrase continuing. Nevertheless they may need adult intervention sometimes in the form of a distraction to help them to wait. Once it becomes a habit, they can manage their patience levels a bit more as they know what to expect.

Teenagers will often say, 'I'm bored,' because they have (apparently) exhausted all possible avenues of things to do. I remember saying this exact thing to my mum whilst she was reading one afternoon during my primary school years, and I desperately wanted her to take me out. I have always been outgoing and spent most of my childhood exploring the outside world, so it makes sense that I was feeling that way. During a child's early years, we can support them in distracting themselves from trying emotions, helping them to self-sooth and learn to manage their strong impulses.

Sometimes children are so excited to get to a destination that they don't consider everything involved. I take them to places that involve a moderate amount of walking most of the time, and even if the children have chosen where to go, they still complain they are tired. I usually respond with, 'What can we do about that?' Unfortunately, they have to learn that there is no easy alternative to walking and that it has to be done at least

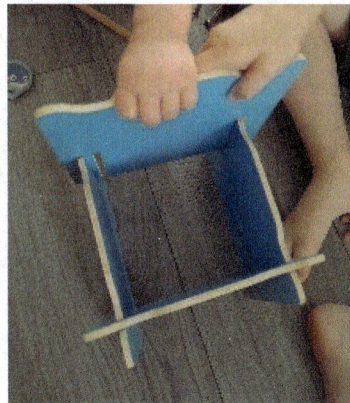

for the time in between public transport. It's not really realistic to say, 'Let's just jump into a taxi' whenever we are tired. I try to teach them about the real world rather than an ideal one. I train them to walk lots, which has always worked wonderfully when balanced with the use of buggies where needed. The older children get a chance to sit, too, if they are very tired, and I let them take turns sitting. This way they slowly develop the ability to walk further. Whilst we walk, we tend to sing or play games which keeps them entertained and distracts them from whining, 'I'm tired.' With parents they will ask to be picked up all the time, but with me they are super-walkers! I tell them they have super-powered legs which motivates them! I also tell them I want to see happy children using their words, not whinging, which they find quite funny! I remember trying to keep up with my fast-walking uncle when I was little, and I got so tired literally running to keep up with him. I try to walk at their pace and tell them to remind me if I start power walking (which I do naturally considering how proactive I am during the day); otherwise, they get exhausted quicker or lose their balance and fall. By encouraging children to walk regularly, we are not only promoting exercise as being healthy, but also teaching them to build stamina, develop patience and the ability to occupy their own minds. In addition, they will learn to observe the details of their environment, keep themselves safe and make the journey fun by distracting themselves if needed.

Other motivators to be active include singing spontaneous songs we have created ourselves. These work wonders and create so much excitement as well as making time pass quickly! Childcare practitioners have to put themselves in children's shoes, imagining what it must be like to walk out into the world whilst we are still learning about it.

Advice and ideas:

- **Encourage children** to do stretches and hold their position for short periods of time, counting the seconds.

- **Meditate together** for a minute or two whilst still and focus on deep breathing. Make sure the children are aware how long this will last.

- If children are able to walk, **take one buggy** and swap who is seated every so often.

- **Be aware of how fast you are walking** and encourage the other children to walk at their friends' pace, too.

- **Sing songs, rhymes and lines** from familiar stories that link to the trip being made.

- **Look around** and spot landmarks, signs and shops; link them to the children's experiences by asking open-ended questions.

· Before leaving the domestic setting, **discuss with the children the logistics of the trip**: where, why and how are all important so they are prepared. This is an opportunity to use time-related language.

• **Avoid feeling the need to constantly distract a child** or try to fill gaps throughout the day; let them get into a habit of thinking for themselves, or even just being comfortable with some quiet time, learning how to wait and deciding what they want to do.

• **Use a stop-watch**, hourglass and/or time-related talk throughout the day to teach them the concept of time.

Reflections

Settling in is much more intense when the parent stays too long; this is because parents' moods are absorbed by children very easily. In my experience it draws out what would have been a quick goodbye. I can understand why parents find it difficult to detach, of course, especially if it's their first child. But saying goodbye at the door makes for a much smoother start to the day. During the first lockdown in 2020 this was trialled out and it has since remained a policy in many childcare settings. It worked very well and still does now. Prospective parents are more than welcome to visit when no other children are present; this is to ensure they have my full attention. Pick-ups and drop-offs are still done at the door, and I try to ensure the children are ready, and then send them out promptly.

In terms of building relationships, children are more likely to feel confident in a situation if parents are. A parent long ago gave my mum a hug and said, 'Aunty, see,' in front of their child; it worked in allowing the child to feel they could also trust her. Children rely on adults to keep them safe and create a sense of security, therefore the feelings being reflected are highly significant.

When an unfamiliar adult comes in and I want the child to build a positive relationship with them, I make sure I am smiley, cheerful and relaxed. This usually gives off an 'it's safe' signal and allows the child to differentiate between a 'stranger' and someone we can trust. When we teach stranger danger or in making children aware of a particular stranger nearby, we will naturally give off a more serious stance. In observing adults' behaviour change depending on context, children can learn how to manage their own feelings as opposed to simply reflecting what they see right back. Sometimes when a parent is telling a child to stop doing something and being extremely strict, children will cheekily completely ignore them and continue being silly. I find however, in this situation there are a few solutions; to move them away from the current setting, to give an ultimatum or to do something completely random and divert their attention immediately. In contrast to being silly with a child or simply giving up, these suggestions will teach children the extent to which following their trusted adult's instructions is important.

Advice and ideas:

- **Role play with friends or family** and practise the drop-off/pick-up interactions you will have with parents.

- **Keep parents updated**, even if with just a few texts or photos throughout the day. Leaving short voice messages/notes is useful on busy days.

- **Don't be afraid of setting boundaries** and only meeting parents out of work hours.

Learning the raw way

We are not robots, we cannot be animated all the time: happy, cheerful and full of energy. Sometimes in a professional or formal situation, despite attempting to put on a brave face, our feelings uncontrollably spill out. One morning just before work I felt so upset because of things going on in my personal life, but I held the tears in when the children arrived. I remember one of the parents telling me it was absolutely fine to cry in front of the children; therefore, I didn't need to say sorry. These days, I am much more open and honest with my feelings, which the children show great empathy towards. I have realised that, in a similar way to the children, we also need to be taken care of! They can sense when I am feeling under the weather or unwell by closely observing my facial expressions. Role playing a range of situations that explore emotions is a great way to get them thinking about how to treat others, exploring possible reactions through improvisation. When I was younger my friends and I loved to play 'mummies and daddies' and now I often join in the children's play with my favourite role being the baby. I act as they do sometimes, and it is so interesting to see their reactions to this. They are learning that people are three dimensional, with different moods and behaviours depending on the circumstances. I encourage them to think about people from all walks of life and represent realistic characters in play whose moods change. They usually use their past experiences of observing others to inform such acting. This is why I think it is very important to show them our true emotions and be as open as we can with our characteristics.

Take a moment

Take a moment to notice the little things: the joys of simple spontaneous events that catch you by surprise and give you that heart-warming feeling, for example, if they say, 'I love you,' or, 'You're the best childminder ever.' I just want to give them a great big squeeze at that moment in time. I will never forget the day I held onto a girl's hand as we ran home in the pouring rain, laughing all the way!

This job allows us to appreciate daily moments in which children are happy leading their own play. I love watching them talking to each other and playing; their interactions developing daily with encouragement and support. Notice how they treat each other with such kindness and care, how they keep play going on their own accord and create their own representations of the world. I love seeing

them acting with consideration of each other and deep empathy, in ways even adults struggle to show. When out on trips, others notice their behaviour, so teaching them appropriate ways to behave does pay off. Building a commendable reputation is an important aspect of childminding and a form of advertising in itself. We have a lot of pressure to act professionally when we take children out on trips and we do get judged; mostly in a positive light is what I have experienced. I have had moments where I did not deal with a situation to the standards of passers-by, however I have learnt from them.

There are parents who let their children play whilst they are fully engaged in a conversation over the phone; I always use these observations to motivate me in getting involved rather than taking a back seat. Childminders have a huge responsibility to set an example for others, whether that may be to prospective parents, other childcare professionals or the children, to inspire people and to go that extra mile in

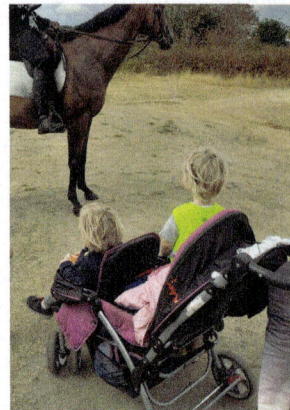

making those in our community proud of us. I am very happy with the positive feedback I've received recently from strangers, who have noticed my efforts and said 'well done' for teaching the kids so well. When I see young children walking hand in hand, showing a heightened awareness of good values and managing their own behaviour, I am so very proud! These are all moments I appreciate.

Keep going!

Settling a child in seems to be more difficult when they have not been to any other such setting previously, especially in relation to their first nap time. It gets easier for children to manage routines over time and so they will learn to sleep independently eventually. Persistence is key for both children and childminders, especially considering the anxiety involved in transitioning to a new setting and getting to know a new child. There are worthwhile long-term benefits to encouraging a child to soothe themselves. It makes perfect sense to take baby steps: you could begin with soothing by singing whilst stroking their head, for example. They may not cry and therefore be content enough to fall asleep independently, however I have never witnessed this for a first nap. Usually there is crying or visible distress of some other kind, but nevertheless I have become confident over the years in using the methods that work. When you find ways of working that you feel comfortable with you can offer suggestions to parents. Whenever I have tried rocking children (even the heavy ones), used a cot, held them and very slowly put them down in an attempt not to wake them. I always seem to go back to the same method of reading a story, kissing them goodnight and leaving the room; in being consistent, bedtime can become a very smooth process. It is a great feeling to know I have taught them to be independent and to self-sooth, as well as influenced their home routine. I understand why parents use dummies and other comfort objects; however, they make more work long term by necessitating more weaning. They also prolong the whole process of children achieving their personal, social and emotional development goals. Instead, parents can focus on simplified methods which you are also comfortable using. The sleep environment should be plain with no distractions at all. That way, they know when they go to that room they sleep and that is all it is used for. Remember, the routines you implement right at the beginning are what the children will become accustomed to. I try to implement rules from day one and keep going with them, making adaptations where necessary where the end goal remains the same.

I have learnt that there are lots of ways to help settle a child, including making a special box of their favourite items, having their most loved toys or activities out, looking at their 'special people' photos together and books related to any of these or even transitions. Providing them with repeated opportunities allows children to build up their familiarity with objects that can bring comfort.

Advice and ideas:

· Be comfortable when working and take on only what you can.

· Rocking a two-year-old to sleep is not going to help anyone.

· Think of long-term benefits when writing your own settling-in policies or putting bedtime routines together.

Empowering young minds

Giving children opportunities to experience activities designed for above their expected stage of development is a great way to challenge and stimulate them. This can be done through finding out a child's potential, rather than allowing them to stay within their comfort zone. A result in hallways being clear of obstacles. child may already be taking an interest in a task that seems advanced, which is where we can get involved. Ofsted do not like the EYFS to be referred to as a check list (during the assessment process) and neither do I. Each child is unique and will achieve according to their individual learning process; for example, a two-year-old's strength may be communication, in comparison to a nearly-three-year-old who has only just begun to speak in sentences. You might have a younger child potty training

at the same time as a slightly older child. Also, each child may not be at comparable levels across different areas of development: a child who is still not able to talk may be physically very advanced.

As a childminder I feel rewarded by letting the children lead and following their interests, observing them closely and planning accordingly. Providing relevant activities and resources sets them up with the tools they need to lead their own play. They need to be in the driving seat to feel empowered; to take responsibility and develop confidence in making choices.

Spontaneous planning

When I first started childminding, I was so focussed on keeping my paperwork up to date that my time with the children had to be compromised. I could never finish all the paperwork I had to do, whereas now I focus only on what is necessary. A fellow childcare professional advised me on prioritising tasks in an action plan, which gave me much more time to spend with the children.

At the time of writing, the recent changes to Ofsted inspections are refreshing to read about because it means a lot less pressure on our shoulders. I hope they keep this ratio of teaching to paperwork emphasis in the future. Activity planning used to always be required in advance and done in the way I was taught from my initial training and experience of working in nurseries—thorough and written with detail. I have since enjoyed spontaneous planning, which involves improvisation and adaptation. I have

learnt that being observant throughout the day helps me to plan purposefully, keeping up to date with the children's interest levels and where they may need extra support. There is also more flexibility when a plan is not so strict. It has taken a lot of experience and skill to plan solely using my mind.

I aim to extend the children's play by giving them 'bubbles' of knowledge (something more in depth in relation to the current activity) to aid their learning and development, for example a fact or a new word. I strongly believe that the impact of this knowledge will depend on the timing of it being initiated; for example introducing a history book during child-led castle role play. Knowing our minded children well means understanding how they learn, having a good understanding of their achievements so far and their goals. This does not mean keeping a written record of every observation, but instead being able to highlight the significant ones. Ofsted want to see that you know your children so well that you can talk about them in

detail when questioned. When I write up observations to send to parents, I make sure I include only specific ones (that will be used for planning next steps), rather than every single one I initially wrote down.

Advice and ideas:

· Invest in a tuff tray for open ended, sensory play; they are accessible and conveniently deep. To begin with, all you need is a simple idea and resources that link in with the current theme or children's current learning goals.

Challenge stimulates growth

Children are unpredictable and, in this job, I've learnt how to create a ripple effect. If an activity is not working, I will change it; if it's too easy, I make it more challenging. It's worth mentioning too that children are sometimes their own best guides to their capabilities. So, I will allow the children to add in resources of their choice and let them choose what to do next. After a demonstration and adult-led activity, I will leave them to lead their own play.

This shows me how much they have learnt and says a lot about their listening and attention to detail, as well as their ability to imitate behaviours. I love to watch how they interpret an activity; their creativity is an insight into their unique minds. These observations of how they learn can then be used

to plan their next steps, with their interests being at the centre.

Children's minds are like sponges; they absorb new information very quickly. Nevertheless they need time to process questions in order to respond. Sometimes when I am not directing all my attention to a specific child, they will complete the task I've been asking them to do for the last five minutes with ease. They often begin with 'You do it,' but I try to encourage them to have a go first. Something I find very interesting is that their actions are highly dependent on who is watching. For example, when parents arrive for pick-up time, the children's personalities often come across completely different than when they're alone with me and are sometimes accompanied by a drastic change in behaviour. This seems to be a combination of excitement to see their parents and the freedom they feel when no longer subjected to a certain routine or set of 'house rules'. In their minds they may be thinking their childminding day is over, so it's time to let it all out. Also, if they have been bound to rules all day, how much longer can they hold it all together? They are experiencing a transition, which can be tricky, especially if they are tired.

The best time to make observations is when children are interacting with each other, particularly to see how they resolve conflicts. In my experience I have found that giving them too much attention means not enough DIY, leading to a lack of self-esteem. If a child is not showing much motivation to be independent, I often ask the family what they do for them at home, and what they have observed from the child. Sometimes I find they are doing everything for the child which links to why they are not showing signs of trying. Learning and development requires teamwork for consistency and to promote new ideas; there should ideally be cooperation between the childminder and child, as well as between parent and childminder.

Advice and ideas:

- Get observations done during child-led play; send them to parents regularly so you each have the child's learning journey within easy access.

You get out what you put in

Going the extra mile means immersing yourself fully into a child's world; making an effort to build a positive relationship and working hard to maintain it. Parents love to see your genuine connection when spending time with their child. For example, during the first meeting with a family, show them you are willing to get down to a child's level and interact in an age-appropriate way; showing an interest.

I find that planning trips to a range of places teaches them about the real world, learning through first-hand, sensory experiences. These opportunities are much more effective than just playing with toys or looking at books, because it supports their holistic learning and cultural capital. It is our job to help them combine both their home life experiences with those from a childcare setting during their critical early years; two integral pieces of their learning and development puzzle. Understanding real world experiences can be represented through role play, through imitating what adults do and what they have observed around them. You can hang up clothes on a washing line together, explore real fruit and vegetables in shopping role play or sing songs in their mother tongue languages.

Each childminder has USPs and so, although having a foundation of core training is essential, to stand out you need to include some extra things in your profile like how your interests and hobbies will positively influence the children. I have always been interested in dance, yoga and fitness, so I implement these into our daily routine. On my childcare profile I focus on my strengths along with ensuring my personality shines through, whilst sounding professional.

I am a firm believer that enthusiasm and passion are needed for a job like childminding, so I would not recommend doing it if those qualities are absent. Experience and qualifications are just as important as attitude and how we come across to others. Parents appreciate childminders who try to be involved in a child's life and often refer to them as a 'second' or 'third parent'. The hard work pays off when we see the relationships we have created flourish.

Self-employment involves managing the business side of things by yourself, but the benefits lie in choosing how to run it. Outstanding childminders are usually willing to go the extra mile because they love what they do. If someone is not fully committed, it is probably due to a change in interest or exhaustion.

I go the extra mile because I love my job and helping families matters to me, as does doing all the extra things that make them glad they chose me as their childminder. There is so much joy in being yourself and using your strengths to your advantage. I have built my business using my love of creativity and my physically active, outgoing nature, and I believe that to run a successful business its core must be one's self. When I need inspiration, I focus on my own capabilities and passions. It is important to remember that children are drawn to our actions, therefore we must involve them in our worldview so they can understand our motivations.

Show and tell

For me, storytelling is not at all about reading in a monotone voice; it's about being creative, adding meaning to the words through body movements, gestures, a range of vocal tones, facial expressions… the list goes on! There is nothing more boring than a book being read with the same tone of voice throughout. Children need visuals, animated voices, a range of sounds and interesting words that are emphasised (for example, a word that is outside of their vocabulary range). Asking them questions and encouraging participation helps them to sit for a longer period of time, rather than wandering off or being easily distracted. I love to capture their full attention and see their smiling faces. There is so much joy in being read to; the excitement builds up throughout in wanting to know what happens next. I feel we have to mirror that excitement to keep the momentum going.

I never carry on a story if children are beginning to fidget; we cannot force children to sit still and focus. I like to ask them questions that link to their

Personal, Social and Emotional development (PSED), to see if they can guess (or remember) what's coming next and count with them, as well as adding in animated expressions. It can be overwhelming to manage a group of children who each have different wants and needs; but a solution is to extend, adapt or repeat activities, in order to be inclusive to all. Having a balance of group and one-to-one activities, is another effective method of teaching so that each child benefits from an equal amount of attention and can make choices in different contexts. For example, if they are being very loud, I suggest we get the instruments out and begin 'music time'; if they are running around, I might direct them to some outdoor time.

Young children are not naturally able to be quiet or sit still for long periods of time, so closely observing and following their lead will keep them stimulated. I tend to move on to the next activity quite quickly if I see them losing interest and this keeps them engaged throughout the day. It's definitely a case of quality rather than quantity and the joys for me personally come from the little snippets of learning taking place.

Stick to your policies

You may come across parents who refuse to abide by your policies, despite signing a declaration to say they will. It's easy to say things on impulse when under pressure, losing all ability to think clearly. But being put on the spot should never be a reason to react, instead it's better to arrange an appointment at a later date, so that matters can be discussed thoroughly face-to-face. I always find that written notes (perhaps in bullet point form) help me to keep on track; ensuring the key points are mentioned.

'No-one can argue against a contract they have signed.' This is what my local childminding group's coordinator has always said: we should be using our policies as our back-up, almost like a shield. In the worst-case scenario, they can terminate the contract without paying the notice period, which is where deposits play a significant role. On the other hand, we can end the relationship, because changing our policies to suit individual preferences is not realistic.

No-one wants to take legal action, so having robust procedures to deal with conflicts is essential and will make clients a lot easier to manage. Partnership working for advice can be very useful in gaining expertise from other childcare professionals.

Being confident and firm in carrying out procedures is the only way to show parents you take your policies seriously; therefore you are less likely to be challenged. We have all been hesitant or too nice at one point or another during our first chapters of childminding.

You must be happy with your clients just as they must be with you; this is especially important at the initial meeting, before anything is signed. Meeting them halfway where it's reasonable and being cooperative is essential but do this without compromising the ethos of your business. For example, work on encouraging parents to speak openly and directly about their concerns as opposed to using other means. If they are not happy with an aspect of your services, address their concerns and reassure them with a positive attitude, even if their requests cannot be totally fulfilled. A little goes a long way sometimes, so it's worth explaining what you can do (if anything), as opposed to just objecting.

There is much to be proud of if you have dealt with difficult scenarios and become stronger as a result, allowing your business-minded self to develop throughout the process. I have found that resilience is needed to succeed with your childminding business, and it will grow.

Roll with the punches

Childminding isn't always smooth sailing; new challenges pop up daily. We all have bad days when we feel everything is going wrong, whether in our personal or work life. However, we have to remember that we are not robots, we have feelings and need to address them. Luckily there is a lot of help and support out there, you just need to be proactive in finding it. When I first began childminding, I was so glad to find my local children's centre; the coordinator and other childminders were so welcoming. I felt like I was a part of something truly significant, doing a job that mattered. Like any self-employed job it takes time to build up any clients at all, let alone a successful business to bring in some financial stability. The groundwork has been training and online research, but having other childminders to speak to face to face on a weekly basis has also helped tremendously. We work alone, which can feel isolating: another reason to join a local childminder network.

You need to be fully committed to supporting families to work in this field, whether you are thinking of childminding or working as a childminder's assistant. There are parents who have no other childcare support, and so need reliability.

When you are passionate about working with children, commitment usually comes naturally and is effective in creating long-lasting attachments. Having said that, it does get easier over time to choose to detach when the children leave, though I absolutely love staying in touch to watch them grow into young adults. They are each unique and certain characteristics they have sometimes remind me of another child, but I have never found the same personality twice. It is challenging to deal with a range of ages and stages of development, however, I have so many fond memories of children being inspired by one another. Children imitate each other and learn both acceptable and non-acceptable behaviour through their peers; there are constant opportunities for

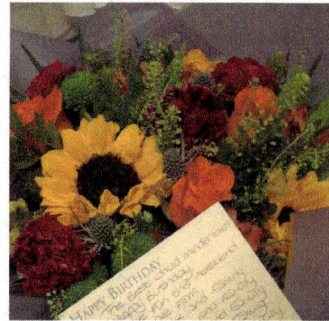

children to differentiate.

One aspect of childminding I truly admire is the appreciation I have received. We (as humans) need to know that we are valued. Personally, I like to read the client reviews and kind words in cards and letters the children have made for me, to make me feel on top of the world again! It is really difficult to switch off your feelings and instead remain 100 per cent business-minded when dealing with anything work related. When your job is a passion, your feelings can get very intense. Self-regulation is key! I often have to remind myself not to get too attached, and instead maintain a balance of meeting the families' needs whilst managing the business side of childminding. This is a learning curve, and it was a long one for me. I once had a parent who would frequently give reasons as to why she could not pay the full week's fees, which led me to eventually terminate the contract. She then asked me to look after the sibling and I only did this for a short time before confronting her like I should have much earlier. Until I spoke to this client's previous childminder who had had the same experience, I thought she genuinely would pay me as promised. I also thought she was going through a rough patch, and that it was a one-off situation. I now realise we cannot work without pay, full stop, and making friends with clients and doing them favours is not an option. Naturally, I felt worried about the family anyway, which led me to put the lack of pay aside. No matter how much advice professionals give, mistakes are inevitable because each business owner will make their own decisions. Considering how many times the children's centre coordinator told our group to always take a deposit, you would think we would listen. But did we? No! We want to help our client families as much as we can, which makes us the caring childminders we are. Wanting to help is a completely natural response, however, there should not be a feeling of guilt as a business owner.

Feeling guilty and wanting to help can make us give in to unreasonable expectations: a completely common and natural process of being a kind person. Now, I would never even dream of looking after a child before a deposit is taken or allowing a parent to use me for a service but not pay. When looking at a situation objectively, it is easier to see the full picture; this is why keeping in regular contact with other childcare professionals is important when working alone.

They will ask

Some parents will ask you all sorts of shady questions in an open and confident way. They might ask for registration details, for example, so they can claim money unlawfully. They will at first appear as though they are asking you to take care of their children… until they say, 'You don't actually need to look after them, we just need your registration details and we can pay you.' They are perfectly aware it's fraud but will try anyway for sure! I have experienced this behaviour on many websites, even the well-known ones, and my response is always, 'No, thank you, because I am a professional childminder.' It is shocking how blunt and direct they can be, considering their illegal aims.

It had never occurred to me that men might set up profiles on childcare sites just so they could lure in childcare workers. The number of times in recent years I have been messaged by single parents who claim to have children who need looking after, stating they have just moved to the area and telling me how much they will pay me. These emails stand out for miles as dodgy and dishonest. I am always relieved when their profiles are deactivated by the website, not long after receiving reports of concern. Having said that, websites like Gumtree, which you would think are less trustworthy, are actually very effective as a form of advertising. I have gained more clients for my dance and fitness classes than I have for childminding, though. There will always be a risk factor of publicity falling into the wrong hands, however, being extra cautious will help protect us. If there are suspicions, not replying straight away is always a good way to give ourselves time to analyse things first.

Men can be childminders

I have worked with both male and female practitioners, and both have been positive experiences; a beautiful partnership that promotes diversity as well as two different styles of role modelling. This combination teaches children that both genders are able to work within childcare with equal competence. Sadly there are more women working in the childcare industry, which may be why some parents are uncomfortable with males doing the same job. However, the children I look after adore having a male role model around. My assistant introduced the punchbag to them and showed them how to use it. It never crossed my mind before to encourage them to use it, but half a year later they are using it frequently. He has a different way of doing things and the children adore him just as much as me; the parents are also happy for us to work together.

I remember how a young colleague, who was often off work, came back into the setting and refused to change any nappies. A child had soiled themselves, and my colleague said, 'Can you do it?' I had been changing nappies all week, so I politely declined, but more to the point I felt annoyed at the fact that she was applying herself to the job half-heartedly.

Through these experiences I have learnt that you cannot choose only the convenient tasks whilst working as a childcare professional; like any other job there are good and not so pleasant parts. Dealing with accidents or dealing with sick children are just a couple I can name. Getting messy and dealing with things outside your comfort zone are inevitable; it's a learning curve.

A bit of struggle builds resilience

In my experience, spoiling and fussing over children will only ever lead to them gaining bad habits or exhibiting unhelpful attention-seeking behaviour. I have found that treating them like little trustworthy and responsible adults will empower them; by showing them you have high expectations, they will thrive. I find it very interesting watching children lead their own play with such confidence and initiative. I have always used the trial-and-error method when it comes to critical thinking; this is also what I teach the children. It is a great way of showing them that persistence is necessary in order to achieve goals independently.

Children will often automatically ask for help without trying first for themselves;

this may be out of habit, because they are used to us doing everything for them. However, praise is a big motivator, encouraging them to develop a 'can do' attitude. Younger children appreciate high-fives, stickers, and other opportunities to be proud of their achievements. It is not always easy to watch a child struggle and wait patiently during their independent learning process. They may whine, cry or simply refuse to persist, but keep in mind that if (and when) they really want to do something, they will. Practice makes perfect; every child is different and some will take longer than others. I find it really interesting how sometimes children who are more than capable will say, 'You do it' or 'I can't do it,' either when they are overtired or feeling lazy. They are children, at the end of the day, so although we want to encourage learning and development, we also need to put ourselves in their shoes sometimes. Crocodile tears that go on and on (or genuine tears that lead to getting themselves more worked up) could be for a number of reasons: because they are overtired, for example, or seeking attention. We all need attention sometimes and a small amount of affection can make all the difference.

If a child is struggling to take off their shoes, I will give a demonstration using simple single words to describe my actions. This helps them to make links and expand their vocabulary. It also helps in breaking a task down for children who are finding it difficult. When a child is learning to put their shoes on, I find that I have to teach them one part at a time, starting with putting their shoes out in front of them, then helping them balance to put their feet in and finally pulling the strap or zip, or tying the laces. They learn and develop skills over time, not when we need them to.

Introducing house rules and routine during their first few weeks with me allows them to learn my expectations of them. Asking them to find their belongings and get themselves ready encourages independence, sets ground rules and teaches life skills. It's not always about focussing on the end goal, but the little tasks involved in the process.

Life is a mix of ups and downs; as human beings, we develop ways of managing our own feelings in appropriate ways. We can gain awareness of how to keep ourselves safe, the confidence to ask for help and the will power to keep on achieving. Hard times make us appreciate the good times and really understand what it means to be happy, to be grateful for the things we do have and can do.

If a child falls down, I encourage them to rub their hands and knees, then get back up using the phrase 'strong boy/girl' as opposed to running to them in panic mode and immediately scooping them up. Nevertheless, asking, 'Are you OK?' shows them you acknowledge the emotional and physical impact of the fall. There will usually be a moment where they look around to see the reactions of the people close by and then decide how to respond accordingly. If there is no commotion they usually get back up straight away without fuss, but if there is tumult then they will usually mirror that feeling: cry at the concerned attention given, or laugh at the laughter they hear. It's much like when I have witnessed fussy eaters refusing food for a while, only to try some when I am not looking! There is no 'one-size fits all' bible, but this is what I have

learnt.

Settling a child in can be anxiety ridden for parents and children as well as nerve-racking for us. Even with the usual, thorough process of finding out as much information on the child, including the 'All About Me' form, home visit and initial meeting, I can never predict how the first week will go.

Children may be clingy during the settling-in period, expecting to be carried or sat on your lap for the whole time. Of course it is necessary to give them comfort, but also to encourage them to explore independently. I usually join in with other children's play and try to stay calm, so they begin to reflect my mood, trust in me and feel secure. Giving them too much attention when they are distressed only leads to further attention-seeking, whereas finding ways to show them how much fun there is to be had, does the opposite.

I have many stories I like to read to the children involving transitions to childcare settings. Many begin with a toddler's negative assumptions about the unknown, but who later on realises it's not so bad after all; this is a very realistic representation. Children will reply, 'No, I want to stay inside' when asked if they'd like to go out, for example, when really, they would have so much fun once they are there! I think of childcare settings in a similar way; until children can focus on the positives, they will not be able to fully appreciate them. I often want to remain within my comfort zone, but when I leave it, I am always glad that I did. The unknown can be worrying; I was always a homely person when I was little, especially when it came to sleepovers. This relates to my introverted self; however, I would never have turned down the opportunity to go outdoors, even now. I was encouraged to be physically active during my childhood years; we spent hours at parks, leisure centres and various sports venues. Getting children to leave the house, however, is not always an easy task as many childcare practitioners will have experienced. Children need time to think and make up their minds, needing guidance to see the full picture of what is to come, before coming to a conclusion. I agree that 'free-flow' (children moving freely between different environments) is important, and that spending lots of time outside is an essential part of children's daily routine for their health and well-being, as well as for learning about the ever-changing world.

I use many yoga and breathing techniques to help calm children down when it's necessary, whether they are distressed due to another child taking their toy, or full of energy during nap time. I hope they can use these techniques on their own accord when needed, throughout their lives. These are some of the foundational life skills they need to learn in order to gain further knowledge and understanding about the world.

Safety and the hands-on approach

I grew up believing I could be or do anything, as many children do, and I still have that mindset now. Taking risks makes me feel challenged, and being out of my comfort zone helps me to learn so much about myself: my abilities, strengths and weaknesses. This is why I whole heartedly believe that if children are given regular opportunities to be physically challenged, they will slowly steer away from their safety net and therefore, will benefit from an increased level of self-esteem. With the children I look after I encourage them to take risks whilst providing a safe and secure environment. In addition (and to help them grow) I ensure they practise movement on as many different surface levels as possible. This encourages them to use their critical thinking skills; planning and assessing their chosen

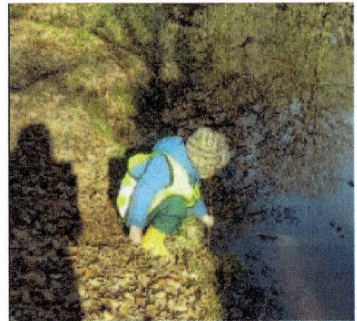

ways of doing things; using trial and error to find solutions. I still remember the first time one of my after-school children climbed all the way to the top of a climbing frame and got stuck. She had climbed it several times before, but this time she eventually shouted, 'Help, I'm stuck!' as she got right to the top. This was the highest she had climbed so far, however, I did not believe she genuinely needed help. The fact that she willingly climbed this huge apparatus was so brave, hence why I let her carry on to the top. When I noticed real tears and saw her panic, I had to stay calm. With a little help I managed to guide her back down and understandably she was shaken. That upsetting experience did not affect her confidence, though, in fact quite the opposite—she began doing gymnastics! From cartwheels to hanging upside down, she learnt it all! Sometimes overcoming a fear happens unexpectedly through an eye-opening experience, ending with a positive step forward. She overcame a fear she didn't know she had, a big achievement in my eyes.

Another time a child in my care took a manageable risk was when a baby attempted to stand on the seat of a tricycle; I stayed close by, but let her do it, and she was so proud of herself, balancing all on her own! She attempted to do other balancing movements after this, so I am very glad I let her do the first one. Following a child's lead is key to helping them develop self-esteem and empowering them in turn. Often, I can see other parents and carers watching and possibly wondering why I am not stepping in to save them. We are the ones in charge and should do only what we feel confident to; we know our children very well and we must have trust in our intuition. Power may be a great thing to have, but the opportunity to empower others is even greater. When we take care of children it's as individuals that we set boundaries, therefore we are directly in charge of the risks children are exposed to. A fantastic way to teach space negotiation is to not intervene when children are moving furniture around in the play room. I often observe children carrying their chairs over to the other side of the table and purposely stop myself from helping; they prove how aware and careful they are in not touching anyone or anything.

One time when out on a trip, I noticed a child on a slide deliberately crashing into my minded children at the bottom, so I made the mum aware. She responded, 'They're only playing,' however there was no care or consideration from her for this behaviour. They were being rough with others and should have known that home and outside behaviours are different; I would not encourage children to behave as this child did when out in public. Children need to know if others are OK with a bit of rough and tumble. In the adult world we wouldn't go up to a stranger and do this, hence why I think teaching them to be considerate of others during the early years is important. More specifically, it is valuable to teach them to wait until the bottom of the slide is clear before they go down, as well as general health and safety principles such as the potential for crushing other children. Healthy habits and social boundaries such as these are difficult to manage when out on trips, due to external factors out of our control. Nevertheless, we can safeguard the children we look after and do the best we can to ensure external factors have a positive impact and deal with negative role models. I take great pride in role modelling and feel the children should too for their peers. Where we cannot eliminate the

negative, we can teach the children about what we see and different social behaviours in context. Identifying hazards and risks is something we talk about daily in our setting to make sure they are not only taught to take care of themselves, but also others.

I know from experience that part of being a childminder is to always be aware of what is happening around us and identify the 'don'ts', like being on our phones whilst the children are left to play. We can make it our business to care about what is happening in the world we live in, not just with our childminding children. I find there is a lot of joy in using my professional judgement—developed through training and experience—to manage childcare issues I see. Knowing what to do in a tricky situation, and having the tools to be able to save a child from further distress or harm, is a responsibility I welcome. I also take pride in, as mentioned above, being aware enough to prevent accidents from happening by doing thorough risk assessments. With other jobs, such as retail and admin work, I always knew what to expect and it was nowhere near as demanding of my energy. I remember operating the till and spacing out but still being able to work as normal; whereas childminding requires a fully focussed, attentive attitude with eyes everywhere. It only takes a second for something to go wrong and therefore is a serious business! Every day is different with childminding which is exactly the way I like it; it's challenging and exciting, therefore I am always learning.

Advice and ideas:

· Take children to various playgrounds that allow them to move in different ways; with a range of surface levels.

· Allow children to feel secure; exploring an apparatus for example, that they have not yet managed to climb, in their own time.

· If a child is reluctant to explore a new apparatus, suggest assisting them the first few times before stepping back and observing the impact.

Fears

Sometimes it's necessary to add some light-hearted humour and fun into everyday routines, like dancing whilst using a blender to make a smoothie when I notice the little ones look anxious at the noise. Teaching them life skills such as cooking is also important, giving them opportunities to develop their concentration, to follow instructions capably and to take an interest in creating something from scratch. Learning practical skills like this can alleviate a worried mind. There is safety and hygiene to consider as well as measuring; the children will learn so much from something adults do daily. The more they get involved, the more they learn and become less reliant on us, the child carers. It does not matter how simple or quick of a task I am showing them; I always make sure that I talk through my actions so they learn through verbal cues as well as visuals. Avoiding doing the things they do not like will not usually help, instead I tend to repeat them more regularly. I also find letting them know the next stage of the routine in advance is important so that they can prepare emotionally for what is coming. Children need reassurance and so do we as adults; therefore, events that happen suddenly throw us off guard. Sometimes panic can override the activity, so making it fun takes that away.

Talking of fears, we have squishy animals in our playroom which a few children have been scared to touch. I just let them explore in their own time; there is no need to make children do anything they do no not want to, especially to the extent of extreme distress. I was once pressured to go into the deep end of a pool by an old friend, and I fell into a state of shock because I was not expecting to and had a fear of deep water. There was no empathy or understanding from them, so I just felt angry. Swimming lessons at school were a completely different ball game as I had reassuring teachers with me every step of the way, as well as other children in the same boat as me. With different ability levels separated, I felt I could progress at my own rate. Children need to feel they have this time, with their teacher being supportive and patient.

If children do not like something I make sure to tell them about it in advance and try to help them through it as much as possible: distracting them, using positive affirmations and comforting them if needed.

I remember the first time my mum left me at reception class; it felt as if someone had pulled my heart out! I have a clear visual recollection of reading Brown Bear, Brown Bear, What Do You See?, only to turn around when it was finished to find she was gone. Previously, she had left me at my cousins' and aunties' houses loads of times, but it was upsetting all the same. To leave your child is one thing, but to not explain what is going on is worse. When childminding, I always ask that the parent says goodbye with a simple reassurance, such as: 'Mummy will pick you up later.' Preparing a child helps them to manage their feelings and know what to expect next. They may still be upset at the time it happens, but at least they will have had time to process the information. They can use this time to manage their emotions by talking about it if they like or having some cuddle time. However, sometimes children

need distraction as well as the explanation. Sometimes nothing we present them with will be of interest, because they will only begin to accept their new setting when ready. It's our job to support a child through their transition process, through accepting their individual needs.

In terms of said distractions, when I drop something that startles them, or when I hurt myself falling over (though not if it's serious of course), I often say 'crash, bang, wallop' which moves them to laughter. If you know your children well, you will quickly notice changes in facial expressions and what each one means. Using silly phrases really lightens the mood. The children I currently childmind have grown out of their fear of loud noises very quickly. This is because I have directed their attention towards fun ideas that link to the noise, rather than any negative aspect. I find that movement is a big distraction for children when it comes to many things, from settling-in anxiety to phobias. When I am using a hand-mixer for example, I shake my body and head which makes the children laugh as opposed to scaring them, as well as giving them advance notice so they can begin to manage their emotions without the shock.

The big transition

Settling a child into a setting is unpredictable because each child is unique and until we get to know them, we cannot know exactly how to meet their needs. Therefore, external factors such as other carers and adults in their life, and any transitions that are going on or have happened, all need to be found out before they begin with you. I consider their home routines so that I can understand how to support them through the transition process. In turn, a setting's routine needs to be communicated to the parent and implemented from the first date of care. I try my best to be consistent, with some room for flexibility, as they get used to a new environment bit by bit. If details regarding their home routine are not given in the registration forms, I ask parents to send them to me in writing as soon as they can. The home visit is usually done within the first month; the perfect chance to get to know the family within their everyday environment. Inclusion, in terms of allowing all types of personality and ability to flourish uniquely, is an important aspect of childminding practise, and children's needs will change as they grow;

therefore, a setting's routine should never be engraved in stone.

The time of day I usually suggest for settling in is first thing in the morning or after a nap, when they will be the least tired. Transitioning to another setting where they can just play is a good first step before trying nap time. A successful transition (ending with a child who is fully settled) could take two weeks of hourly visits from me, or just one week followed by full days during the second week. Some children will fall asleep even as they are slightly distressed, others will want to sit in their buggy for comfort. Therefore, during the settling in period, we must ensure children bring in comfort items such as familiar blankets, an item of clothing with a familiar scent, or a favourite soft toy. These will help children to self-soothe as a result of feeling safe.

You need to put in the hard work for both you and the children to enjoy the many benefits. This responsibility and the development of relevant skills, such as assertiveness, are joys of childminding, as is going the extra mile from the very start of relationship-forming and seeing these connections blossom.

The proactive parents

There are parents who enjoy getting stuck into arts and crafts projects with their children, which is refreshing to see. Even as they find it very helpful when I suggest simple, quick activities to try at home with their kids, not all have the time or energy for it. I can completely understand how difficult it must be to fit everything in when you have children and a busy working life. Those that do, however, give me so many ideas and inspiration too! When I do home visits these really jump out at me, especially when their crafting is out of this world, from making their own tepees to Halloween treasure boxes. It just goes to show that it does not matter how much money a family has, they can build something out of nothing! Natural resources are all around us, as are household objects; these can be used for heuristic play or to build something bigger.

Heuristic play provides sensory exploration for young children and babies and it involves putting household or natural objects found outdoors, in a textured basket. Some examples include acorns and cleaning brushes; which spark curiosity and encourages focussed play that lasts a long time, and allow all the senses to be used. During this type of play, it is important that adults simply observe and allow the child to investigate independently. Something I often see parents doing at home is giving their children pots and pans to make music, making dens out of sticks and cloth, and decorations from cupcake cases dangling from hangers.

I think it's wonderful to walk into a house that has clearly been loved and lived in without fear of being chaotic; where you can see children are at the heart of the action. I love seeing how families utilise a space, prioritising what will be accessible to their children. There's so much joy in noticing what's around us and allowing others' creative spaces inspire our own.

At the table

There are many great bonding moments throughout the day for the children and I, including meal times, when we have eye contact and can focus on one another. At the table, we discuss what we will be doing later or how their weekend was, anything that is appropriate for the duration, and I ensure they put toys, books and media away to avoid distractions. We have music on so long as it serves a purpose, linking to the current activity or a child's request. There is no way I would get them into the habit of watching something whilst they eat, even for convenience or a last resort.

Speaking of media, I once worked as a live-out nanny for a boy who would not eat unless he was watching something; so, his family would use it as a distraction to feed him. He was a very fussy eater, or so I was told, but I did not learn anything about his likes or dislikes through his behaviour. I began encouraging him to explore foods as a way of weaning him off technology. I had never seen a three-year-old drinking from a baby bottle before, nor having all his cutlery sterilised thoroughly or being changed on a mat. I encouraged independence and set boundaries, taking him out every day and doing lots of one-to-one focussed activities. He was well and truly the 'king of the house', hence why the parents called me in to help. They knew changes had to be made but needed help to break the cycle. The parents agreed he was very intelligent, but they needed me to help manage his PSED due to their demanding jobs. They hardly saw their son: maybe for one day a week at most.

Over time, I felt uncomfortable adapting to the family's rules, and I am much happier with my role as a childminder now. Where a family do not change their habits to fit with a child's developmental needs, it will make consistency more difficult to attain. This means the child will make progress whilst in my care, but then go back to their old ways when with their family.

Despite these challenges, he was a changed boy by the end of that month, so I am extremely proud of myself for the methods I used! I feel frustrated when children's development is hindered; sometimes it seems that parents are not motivated enough to adapt current routines, whether lacking knowledge on how to support their child or overwhelmed by a busy schedule. Convenience should never be the reason we (practitioners and parents) do not show an interest in a child's development. In Putting the EYFS Curriculum into Practice, Alison Peacock discusses the importance of the parent/carer and educator role (Peacock, 2023, 192–193). She states that back-and-forth interactions between child and carer are fundamental, as is receiving support from an educator: someone who has the professional knowledge to expand a child's thinking. In light of this, where there are barriers within their home learning, they can work with parents to achieve a consistent approach. Dummies, for example, are a very convenient comfort item, however, they stop children from communicating. As Peacock goes on to explain, children have a desire to communicate, as well as the need to be heard (Peacock 2023). This suggests that

we should be adapting the environment according to their needs, instead of putting routines in place that are convenient for us. In working closely with families, we can exchange ideas and observations so that the child can reach their full potential. It's not just about providing age-appropriate resources or lots of books, but fundamentally about the way we communicate with them and keep that going.

Something that really comes to mind when thinking about Peacock's theory on the roles of parents is witnessing children completely glued to a tablet whilst eating out with their family! I have seen that taste changes over time (naturally) and the opportunities we offer can directly influence children. I think it is important to be aware of our body language along with the verbal language we use, for example, by exploring out loud the textures and flavours of food with an eager, positive and open, 'don't-know-unless-you-try' attitude. We can change our menus week by week and cook familiar or multicultural food liked by families, so that our setting's mealtimes are diverse. It's perfectly OK for children to dislike foods, so long as they are open to trying new things. If we do not encourage children to explore world foods whilst they are in their early years, they are more susceptible to developing fussy attitudes.

I can understand that parents sometimes just want a peaceful evening and a bit of a break too, however, it is sad to see a lack of conversation at the table in the spirit of 'family time'. One of the aspects of having a family I am really looking forward to is meal times so we can sit together and talk. I love talking to children about textures, tastes and food in general, asking them questions like, what does it smell like? We must make meal times fun and exciting, so that they anticipate it within our routine. Bribes lead to tantrums, emotional meltdowns and repeated unacceptable behaviour, so it may seem convenient at the time, but long-term difficulties will arise, just like when I experienced the little boy only eating if the television was on. Feeding children facts at meal times can be both educational and motivating, which is another reason to have discussions around the table. I have seen children go from fussy eaters to very good eaters, just by teaching them what is in their food, how it is made, and so on.

Many parents give out snacks to keep their child in the buggy, or just to keep them quiet, for that matter, which the children get used to. I looked after a toddler years ago who would expect Mum to bring a sweet snack every day with her at pick-up, because she usually did. When she did not, there was most definitely a tantrum! Sitting still at a table, focussing on food and showing good table manners is a lot to expect from a child in the early years. One step at a time and they can get there, with the help of both the parents and childcare practitioners.

There are challenges nevertheless, and ways of managing these situations, also. I find it interesting that there is always one child talking at the table whilst the rest are quietly chewing away. If they are becoming disruptive or fidgety, I sometimes read to them, which they absolutely love! If I find they are getting bored of sitting for long periods, I engage with them to make sure they have eaten enough. Children with a low attention span may need further encouragement, so I make sure I sit next to them and make the experience a positive one. I once had to leave the playroom during lunch time to sit on the bottom stair with a child who would just leave the table after a few bites of his food, looking sad. This is a good example of when adaptations need to be made by identifying the child's need, making sure we listen attentively, as Peacock states above. The fact that he would happily eat all his food on the step makes me think that maybe he just needed some one-on-one attention and some quiet time. There are many children I have come across who are extremely sensitive to noise, and they can be given encouragement to find a quiet space when they need to. I find great joy in empowering a child; by allowing them to choose how, what and when, as opposed to deciding for them. Before they are confident and content in their environment, how can we move on to other things? The foundation to their learning and development is their self-care and ability to be confident; this is how they thrive. There is so much joy in learning from a range of eating habits and meal time scenarios, updating our skills and knowledge, then passing it all on to the parents.

Bye-bye nappies, hello pants!

Using fun catchy phrases will help children to achieve their next steps, especially if they have fears that form barriers. It makes the whole transition process seem fun and positive!

Once they begin to make these positive links they can move forward with optimism. Children often become so comfortable with wearing nappies that when it comes to sitting on a potty or toilet, they are scared to do poos. I remember being scared of the toilets in my nursery class, because of the noise of the flush and the toilet itself. We as adults know there is nothing to be scared of really, but bathrooms can be so noisy and to make it worse each one is different. The main fear I have observed in children is that of falling into the toilet. This is why I begin with baby steps rather than a plan that means we have to tick each goal off within a certain timeframe. Many parents take two weeks off and focus on potty training at home consistently, which works if we as childcare practitioners can carry on with it.

We should be mindful that some children use the potty first and some head straight to the toilet. Regardless, I begin helping them with themed books, then role play using dolls or small world figures and encourage them to talk about their friends who are already more independent with going to poo or wee. I usually use the 'Zoom Zoom Zoom, We're Going to the Moon' song and change the lyrics to make it relevant for toilet time—they find it really funny! It adds some fun and hopefully builds on their ability to be resilient, turning something negative or anxiety ridden into something positive.

When all my childminding children are of similar age groups and stages of development in terms of toileting, we reserve specific times for using the bathroom. This way they learn the importance of regular toileting—enhanced by discussing how the kidneys are affected if we hold urine in. Life transitions, such as a new sibling or baby in the family, for example, can affect a child's stage of development, causing regression. During this phase they are likely to need reminders throughout the day, even if they have been very good at going for several months. The other thing to remember is sometimes children think they do not need to go, but actually they do, therefore before trips, I always make sure we try. Despite the above toileting routine, the overall aim is for the children to regularly use the toilet throughout the day, independently. Accidents happen, however, and I am very aware of how a child's self-esteem can be affected, especially if those accidents are recurring. There are children who will just ask for new trousers, not really focussing on what has happened at all, in comparison to children who will cry their eyes out and I can clearly see they feel disappointed in themselves. These latter children in particular need a routine: it really helps them to get back on track to move forwards rather than regress.

Children gain motivation through observing their peers: something I have noticed in relation to toilet training. I encourage the joy of being proud and supportive of others' achievements: to praise our peers and give a helping hand or demonstrate where we can. We clap for each other and acknowledge when our friends have a 'wow moment'. There is so much joy in encouraging children to achieve with and alongside others rather than against them; it does not have to be a competition! In helping others to reach their goals, one can still be successful.

Knowing your children

I used to spend so long trying to memorise a child's personal information, routines, date of birth, etc, which of course are important. However, I now realise it's more about knowing their personalities! I have learnt that it's a case of predicting what they will do before they do it, by making observations that help us to identify patterns in their behaviour.

It's about keeping in mind their current stage of development and being able to explain where their learning is taking them; their characteristics; how they choose to play and their repeated behaviour (or schemas); their chosen way of playing. As childcare practitioners, it's about being able to step into their shoes. I find the more time we spend getting to know our children, the closer our bond becomes, and the more they exceed expected outcomes.

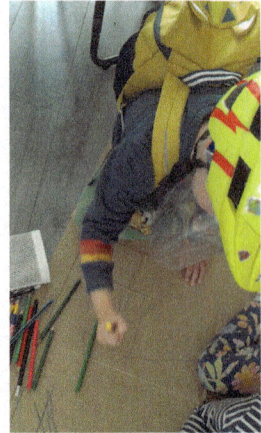

They can be quicker learners when we take time to identify what they need and where they are headed, which is why making observations is the first step to planning. Children achieve so much more when we act on their interests at the time they are expressed, whilst we continue to think about their next steps. Having said this, it's crucial we do not miss opportunities to spend quality time exploring with children and being immersed in the moment, rather than simply ticking off each goal once achieved. I have learnt over the years that we do not need mountains of paperwork to prove we run outstanding settings; the proof is in what can be witnessed from the children and staff, in other words, how visibly effective the teaching and environment actually are.

They can and they will!

Each child will develop at their own pace; this means some may pick things up quicker than others. The main thing to remember is when you give them encouragement, they will be more motivated to keep on trying. Show them unconditional love, even if they fail numerous times or struggle—and you think they maybe can't manage something—and give them a chance. We all get a bit frustrated and tired at times, but children need our commitment and positive reinforcement. I always leave a little extra time in the day to encourage child-led tasks, which takes thorough planning and organisation. Some childminders (like those in schools) are very strict with their timings for each day, however, with children coming in and leaving at various times I find it a lot easier to be flexible. I plan based on which children I have to provide for and their individual needs.

I prefer to be strict when it comes to teaching children consequences, because I have found that they learn best when they have no other options. For example, we don't begin snack or meal time until the playroom is tidy; if a child makes a mess, they clean it up, including the sand in the garden (which always ends up on the turf); and if they drop something they pick it up. Sometimes they just don't want to do things for themselves, but begin to once they realise they have to in order to move onto the next part of the routine.

When children learn to claim responsibility for their own actions, they become considerate for the world and people around them and much more aware of things they maybe should not do. They learn from previous experiences of having to spend ages cleaning or tidying up, and so choose not to repeat mistakes.

Your little helpers

Children love responsibility: whether you are asking them to sweep the floor or stack their chairs. So if a child loves construction you could ask them to fit the table legs on the table—with supervision of course. If they are seen playing with cleaning utensils, you can ask them to tidy their play kitchen. Teaching children life skills such as DIY and taking care of themselves will have a significant impact on their independence and habits. For children who have extra energy or show attention-seeking behaviour, it's about teaching them how acceptable behaviour can be more rewarding. Looking closely at schemas will help us to plan for their individual needs; if we see children lining things up for example (creating linear structures), they are practising transferable skills necessary for other contexts

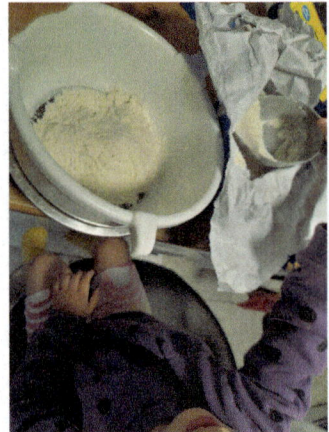

in life. Think about the level of accuracy and concentration needed not only to build a straight line, but also to create a sequence. This child-led activity can help develop the ability to organise kitchen utensils and bottles of herbs.

Ensuring children take some responsibility has been embedded into our daily routines, so that children learn the sequence of how we do things. For example, before we sit down to eat, we tidy up; after eating, we take our cutlery to the kitchen sink. They absolutely love helping to clean and tidy, even if it's just a few little tasks. They are learning to differentiate between what adults do and what children are allowed to do, as well as what they need permission to do. The antibacterial spray, for example, is only ever used by an adult, whereas the water spray children can use. Expectations must be realistic; so I sweep first and then give them a chance to do the rest. I can be just as proud of a child tidying up a few toys, as I would be for an older child who tidies a whole section of the playroom.

Children need encouragement to build positive relationships not just with other children, but with adults too. By setting boundaries we can earn their respect; therefore, implementing house rules is very important and can benefit everyone. The children need to learn that leaving their belongings scattered all over the floor and expecting adults to pick them up is not a realistic expectation to hold, and that being tidy is a helpful behaviour. If they are to step on toys that are on the floor, break things or pull down display work, then this requires taking responsibility and children need to see the consequences that follow. These consequences then make them more aware that there should be a thinking process before the actual doing. Risk assessments are very effective daily tasks to do with children, allowing them to understand the importance of planning in advance. Children are learning the 'why' rather than being repeatedly told 'Because I said so' or 'No means no.' Activities involving the assessment of risks and hazards can challenge children, encouraging them to think about how their environment needs to be managed and what the consequences would be if they were inattentive. They enjoy these tasks because they see us doing them, so involving them will have a positive impact on their learning and development.

We have enough time to 'baby' them, make sure they are taken extra good care of and do tasks for them; therefore, there comes a point in their early years when we must encourage a stricter routine. Being responsible is a part of growing up; something I truly learnt when moving out of my family home. However, I know for sure that everything I learnt growing up is now a part of my daily routine, including life skills. Children will be much more prepared to be independent if we teach them how to be self-sufficient rather than depending on us all the time. I believe that children will rebel if overprotected (as I was), whereas stepping back gives them more opportunities to manage their own behaviour, think of others' needs and cooperate. Teaching children to help with daily chores will eventually result in tidying and cleaning on their own accord, rather than being reminded frequently. We simply need to encourage child-led play so that they can develop life skills, and build on their fascinations of the world.

Role models

If you have been around children, you will notice that they imitate grownups, adapting their personalities according to what we say and do; therefore, children benefit from positive role modelling. One of the things that Ofsted picked up on during my last inspection was that I am a positive role model; I am very aware of everything I say and do. Nevertheless we all slip up sometimes when communicating and get our words twisted, so correcting our mistakes is very important. My weakness is definitely pronouncing big words, but to help children learn correct pronunciation we can break words down into syllables. In a similar way, when children say things too quickly, I ask them to repeat themselves. We must demonstrate what we say and do clearly, to ensure children understand correctly, and help them to do the same.

I will say something back to a child in the correct

way, perhaps adding words to their original sentences, say, or demonstrating good manners. Teaching them to adapt to their environment is important too, for example, being quiet during nap time and going outdoors to run around.

Another important job of ours is to ensure our actions abide by our settings ethos; for example eating healthy in front of the children, which is positive role modelling. In contrast eating crisps whilst they are eating their lunch is not going to motivate them much at all.

Helping children to differentiate between acceptable and unacceptable behaviour, to be kind and considerate towards others and to respect rules in context are some of my main priorities. The joy for me lies in spreading my enthusiasm for learning, so that they adopt the same traits and are motivated to learn. This will lead them to keep on building on their knowledge and be successful in life.

Use your contacts to refresh your thinking

With so many channels for childminders to communicate via and use for research, we can easily gather new ideas and find inspiration for creative projects to keep the children stimulated. As opposed to repeating the same activities all the time, we can try out new ones that link in with a current theme.

It is quick and easy to join a childminding Facebook group. You can also make it a habit to be in touch with the local children's centre and network with others when out on trips. Our bond as a childminder network is strengthened with regular meetups outside of the centre, which make me feel as if I have both my friends' and my colleagues' continued support. Networking helps you grow as a business; the more contacts we have, the better our opportunities. It is very useful to exchange experiences and learn from fresh perspectives. With that said, it is not a case of letting everything others say influence you, because each childminder has individual ways of working. However, asking for some help or finding the positives together are key parts of our Continuing

Professional Development (CPD). There is so much inspiration to be found around us! Sharing my level of expertise and listening to others is definitely one of the things I love about networking.

Working in partnership with other professionals to share information about a child is an important aspect of childminding. To fully understand a child's behaviour, we need to first find out about other settings they visit regularly and collect any observations from their parents or carers; the same goes for any previous childcare settings. It is important to ask parents questions about their children; children are usually very different at home to the way they are within a childcare setting. For example, I give them a particular and structured routine along with a set of specific rules, and the children see me as a teacher-like figure as opposed to a parent.

Getting an insight into a child's home life is beneficial for all the above reasons. I am always interested to learn about families through regular conversations; this helps me to know how best to support the child.

Networking however, is also about thinking of ways to create long lasting connections with the local services; giving children an invaluable learning experience that is close-up and sensory. This is an opportunity for the children to ask questions and for us to learn alongside them as opposed to being the teachers. Not only will they gain knowledge for their own aspirations, they will learn exactly what specific job roles entail and therefore be far more appreciative. We send thank you cards to all who have played a part in meeting with us; so far we have in depth sessions with firefighters, train staff, paediatrics, and the local dental team. To ensure children notice the hard work of those in our community, we stop and talk to the people others may simply walk past, including street cleaners. These insights teach them that everyone has an important role to play in our community.

Generally and on a day-to-day basis, we can work with other settings that our minded children attend; to exchange developmental information. For advice on safeguarding matters I know that I can contact MASH (the Multi Agency Safeguarding Hub). If there are concerns involving a child who has additional needs/extra support, the local SENCO (Special Needs Education Coordinator) can be contacted. They may visit a setting to observe children closely, so they can identify exactly what kind of help is needed.

It is very reassuring to know that there are local teams available to help and within easy reach; they provide a diverse range of expertise, that do fall within a childminder's job role. In gathering information, we are using a holistic approach for the benefit of the child.

Think about your individuality; use your strengths

Think about what you can offer families that will make you stand out. A lot of childminders drive, for example, or do multiple school pick-ups, both of which can be appealing for families. Everyone has something unique to offer, whether it's dance, tuition, childcare outside of sociable hours or the ability to speak different languages. These things demonstrate extra effort in addition to the common services offered.

Do you provide nutritious, home-cooked food, diverse outings and resources, or adaptations for SEN (Special Educational Needs) children? These extra things should be highlighted on your profile when advertising: together they will form your USP to attract clients. When families come to visit your setting make sure to mention these, as well as showing them the children's special

books with permission) and certificates for non-core courses. Special books (also known as learning journeys) showcase a child's development from beginning to end in chronological order; including their artwork, photos, and observations. Children and their parents love to look at these on a regular basis and help to design them, too. When children leave, they have a collection of their achievements to take with them and treasure. In this modern world, with the EYFS guidance being updated regularly, it is important we remember why we make efforts to grow our skillsets in the first place.

As a childminding setting is run solely by you, the business owner, you can choose whether to carry on providing these extras because it is beneficial to your families, or just to do what is necessary. There are so many things we do not have to do, but I personally love to focus on the things that make my setting that extra bit special—what families will appreciate, remember and treasure. I can understand why some settings charge more than others because of the services offered. It may also just be a case of what people will pay in a specific location, but nevertheless, I know from experience that if you fulfil a family's requirements and then some, parents will choose to go with you. No matter how much less than the market average a childminder is charging, or how much closer they live to the client family, parents can still be extremely particular in choosing what suits their needs the best, particularly with how many childcare settings there are around. They will travel further and pay more for what they want rather than settling for less, and I believe I would do the same for my children. It is a bit similar to shopping, for example, buying something cheap that you do not really want, versus travelling a bit further to buy another item that you love. Your charges will also reflect your situation and circumstances; you may simply not feel the need to charge more than the average because you are happy enough. Some childminders are not able to increase their fees because the average charge in their location is not as high. Helping families is also important so if I know a family really like my setting, I will try my best to adjust my usual fees.

Demonstrate and move on

Sometimes demonstrating appropriate behaviour has more of an impact than to focus too heavily and continuously on mistakes the child has already made. It's great to focus on the matter briefly at the time, then ask them to rectify their mistake with a 'sorry' (if appropriate) and a hug. Nevertheless they sometimes refuse to cooperate in the moment, and therefore need some thinking time. I always find that as long as you are teaching them what they should be doing according to house rules, the child will respond appropriately or do as instructed, given this time to remember. If you keep them talking about the incident, they may just repeat the same undesirable behaviour, because you are not giving them the opportunity to change. Labelling them with their misdemeanours, or continuing to judge them despite new and desirable behaviour, is not going to help them develop. They need to know that once there has been closure and resolution, they have the opportunity to do better; in our eyes we love them unconditionally and have faith in their ability to develop. Feeling resented is a horrible feeling to live with. One time a nearly-three-year-old went to the toilet independently but took way too much toilet paper and I found he'd put the excess in the bin when I checked on him. Since then, I have often used the word 'trust' when I talk to him; fortunately, he takes responsibility seriously and has not repeated the behaviour since. Children want to be trusted because they want to manage their own responsibilities and feel more in control. I find much joy in showing a child I believe in and think very highly of them, which is why when I hear 'I can't,' I refuse to accept it.

The unacceptable behaviour cycle

It takes years of experience to be able to simultaneously balance managing a setting with understanding a child's point of view. If a child is kicking something they should not be, for example, I would just direct them to something they can kick, like a ball. If they are running around the room or pushing a buggy around with no clear motive, they perhaps need to go outside where they have more space! It is easy to get into a cycle of addressing the unacceptable behaviour, giving an explanation of the negative consequences, then ending up repeating the whole process again. I find it more effective to give the child an ultimatum, as even if they begin having a meltdown or resist making a decision, I can then follow through with an action. Children focus on things they are interested in, therefore there is an opportunity here for teaching: we can let them continue their play but in a more appropriate context. I remember when I was a teenager thinking, 'It's not fair' and feeling trapped whenever I heard 'Don't' or 'You can't.' Children and young people can be headstrong once they make up their minds, showing us their urge to be empowered. No-one responds well to being restricted, therefore children are much more likely to compromise if we give them choices. The root cause for their behaviour also needs to be addressed so we can work to fulfil their needs.

Not everyone is comfortable with letting children make a mess or be noisy. It's important to think about ways in which we can be inspired by their characteristics to plan activities, or how we can take them somewhere they are less restricted and feel appropriately challenged. Their behaviour will be no longer about attention-seeking then, and instead more about achieving a goal.

Schemas are helpful in that they guide us to understand children's repeated behaviour, thereafter we can plan activities based on this link between motivation and action. For example, if a child is frequently scattering bangles… rather than assuming they are just deliberately making a mess, we can give them something else with a sensory quality they can scatter, or dice. Scooping and pouring activities can be appealing to children who love emptying toy boxes out. To actively share in a child's interests even when they are going about them in the wrong way is something that keeps me on my toes and challenges me, but something I enjoy doing.

'Because I said so!'

Saying 'no' can become an automatic response, whether to children doing something dangerous or something we think is unacceptable. I try to encourage them to be aware of what they are doing, identifying what it is first and foremost. Saying 'stop' or using another simple phrase for an immediate reaction is better than 'no' being frequently used. The more you use it the less effective it becomes. For example, a two-and-half-year-old begins scattering bangles on the floor a handful at a time, looks at me, then grabs more. I let him finish and make sure he tidies up before he gets out a new toy, then I explain why we must tidy up in the first place. They need to learn the reason for rules. When babies or young children first come to a childcare setting, they often have no concept of rules yet (let alone rules in context), but after a short while they develop the ability to follow them through, if you are consistent with reminders. If you tidy up after them and do not enforce boundaries, they will go into the world thinking they can do whatever they please. It is our job to teach them what kind of behaviour is socially acceptable and appropriate, according to rules in context. In contrast, however, too many rules can make children feel trapped!

I find that a child will often learn more from experiences without any intervening instructions from me like saying 'stop'—through accidents, for example, that are inevitable. A parent once told me that even though she predicted her daughter would fall before it actually happened, she did not stop her. Her toddler began jumping in the shower cubicle, but Mum did not intervene, instead she froze. When the little girl did fall and cry, Mum felt extremely guilty. We know the children we look after very well and when to intervene, but also when to give them their freedom. It gives me a sense of pride when I allow children to test out their ideas; this allows me to understand their level of awareness of how to keep themselves safe. If the consequence of their actions will harm them, then of course we should step in immediately and ensure their next steps link to those observations.

I find it hard to see people close to me get hurt, especially when I can predict what will happen. On the other hand, sometimes we think we know an outcome, but the situation turns out completely differently. We often have no choice but to let people go through things even if they are not pleasant experiences. The main thing is that they learn from their mistakes; children can make their own choices and should face consequences so they can learn. Each individual childcare practitioner will need to decide to what extent they allow children to explore, before stepping in. We cannot in any capacity stop people from making choices, but we can intervene where necessary. Our job is not to rush to their aid to stop any kind of fall from happening; we can however have rules in place and teach them how to risk assess, as well as provide them with a child-friendly environment. Safeguarding is of course a priority, but we should also offer opportunities for trial and error, risk-taking, etc.

Advice and ideas:

- Stick different ways of saying things on the wall for assistants and yourself, such as 'What will happen if...?', 'Maybe we can...' or 'Is that a good idea?'

Not for the squeamish

Sensory play offers endless opportunities for children to explore through sight, touch, smell, hearing and taste. The wider the range of media and materials you have at your disposal, the better they are for the children's learning. This does not mean having tons of different things as such, but instead 'loose parts' (gems/shells/pasta/lolly sticks) in a range of sizes, colours and textures. Sensory play can go on for a long time with only a small number of resources.

There are so many words that can be used to describe not only textures but also actions of manipulation, for example: sticky, gooey, kneading, poking. In order to implement this teaching, practitioners must join in with the activities to encourage participation. Not all children will have a go, and some may not know how to use the

resources, for example, if it is their first time. To avoid conflicts, boredom or inappropriate use of resources, an adult must be proactive in participating and be close by at all times.

Considering how significant the practitioner's role is in such play, I know that watching from a distance does not have the same effect. I understand there are people who do not like getting their hands dirty and children can be the same at first; it takes some getting used to. I remember working at a pre-school as a trainee not knowing what to say or do. I thought the staff set up the water activity for the children to play independently and my role was just to supervise, staying close in case they needed me. I now understand the significance of being involved in their play, to guide, demonstrate and expand their vocabulary.

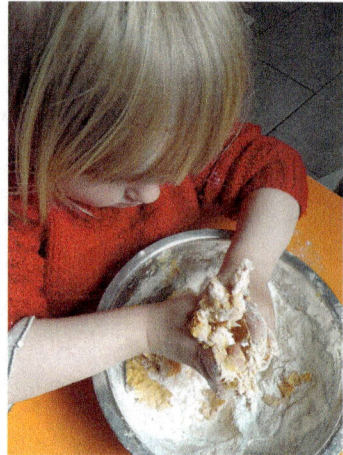

I can see how far I have come when I look back to my traineeship; these days, by bedtime I have sand in my hair (that's all, if I'm lucky), slobber on my clothes and have been inevitably sneezed or coughed on repeatedly. Children should be free to use their whole bodies to explore and so should we! Showing them our excitement will usually take the fear aspect away for the child. Parents understand that we take the supervision of children seriously and do not use phones unless necessary: photos and observations come second to being involved.

As long as parents provide spare clothes and do not bring them in wearing their best, getting messy is not an issue. There have only been a handful of times parents have questioned if I am using bibs, because their child's clothes were not clean at pick-up. We do however allow children to eat independently as soon as they are able, so even whilst wearing a bib there is still a possibility their clothes will get messy.

Advice and ideas:

- Use large messy mats, old towels or materials such as sarees to protect your things getting messy. Towels are useful in soaking up water that is spilt; place them under water trays.

- Wear an apron or cheap/old clothes and get stuck into messy play.

- Always have soapy water, wipes or wet towels ready to clean the children up before they touch everything.

- Use sand- or water-filled washing-up gloves (tied at the ends) for those who are not fond of touching sensory materials.

- Ensure parents know their children will get messy in advance, ask for some old clothes and use wipes or washing-up liquid mixed with water for stains, ideally soaking them.

- Use empty drinks containers for sensory bottles and zip-seal food bags to fill with materials such as oil and water, glitter, lentils or jelly.

Invest in a glue gun to prevent children opening them!

· Find, mix and experiment with things round the house like different sized scoops or containers. Scientific looking test tubes encourage filling and emptying; also they are a great tool for teaching mathematical concepts. Measuring jugs will also do the job!

Actions not just ideas

My action plans did not focus on priorities as they should have when I first began childminding; instead, my endless lists resulted in a feeling of overwhelm, through the highlighting of quantity over quality. Also, my life would revolve around work 24/7; I felt like I could not switch off and always had work at the back of my mind. I now realise that the childminding workload is big enough without having the pressure of a million little things to 'complete it'. To maintain a quality setting, it is a case of keeping paperwork updated (as per current legislation), working on CPD, keeping parents satisfied, ensuring effective teaching is happening and, importantly, providing an exciting, safe and secure environment for children. Risk assessing and keeping the house clean and tidy is an ongoing, daily chore. You cannot do everything at once, so it is important to put things in order of priority. This means everything below your top priority is secondary and will only get done once the other items are ticked off. This system allows for more time and effort to be spent on the most important tasks first, so that quality is not disregarded. You have to remind yourself that you are only human at the end of the day, therefore, you cannot possibly do everything, but nevertheless you can manage your time well.

I have learnt to set realistic time scales for goals, ensuring a thorough job is done rather than a rushed one. Everyone has weaknesses and strengths, so when a complaint is made, the best advice I have received is to take each point with a pinch of salt. Most importantly, I try to deal with feedback and concerns with a professional, calm and reflective attitude. As difficult as some of us find it to keep emotional aspects of childminding separate from the others, we must learn how for the sake of professionalism. The more time spent dwelling over situations, the more difficult it becomes to move on.

There are many times we need someone else's advice because everything can become a blur when you are in the same environment constantly. A crucial part of being a successful childminder is to always ask yourself, 'How could I have handled the situation better?' or 'How can I make positive changes within my practise?' Reviewing and evaluating regularly helps me to keep my setting operating to the highest standard, so long as I make sure to put these ideas into action. Safeguarding always comes first alongside adapting to suit individual children's needs, for example, as they change and grow. It is important to look closely at their current age and stage of development and decide whether their environment is suitably stimulating. Everything in your setting, such as displays, units and areas designated for different purposes, should be easily moveable or easily transformed.

Personally speaking, going the extra mile means going on a learning journey together (the child and practitioner) following the child's pace and ensuring they are supported in achieving their developmental milestones. Once you have the basics in place to pass your registration visit, you can take steps to improve and develop your practise for years to come. Even after ten years of childminding I am frequently changing the setting's layout and adding to it; that is what keeps it exciting!

Advice and ideas:

- Keep a notebook for writing down and evaluating feedback to help you reflect and improve.

- Write up and monitor the progress of your short- and long-term goals.

- Write a goal up somewhere in big letters or repeat it to yourself first thing in the morning, so you are motivated to succeed.

- If a task (activity plan/report writing) is not working, step away from it and come back another time.

Give yourself a pat on the back

Praising yourself for what you are doing well is just as important as identifying your weaknesses; continuing professional development should ideally be a balance of both. Even outstanding childminders have things they can work on; maintaining a high standard of care is hard work! I take the children out daily, provide lots of dance and exercise activities, cook meals from scratch, deal with enquires as soon as they come in, constantly clean and tidy throughout the day...; you have to multi-task all the time! On busy days I get a short break or no break at all, and I eat just when I can. It's not ideal, but forgetting to eat and drink is not unusual when you are looking after multiple children. You can however cook meals in advance, cook a batch of food that will last a few days, or cook a bit more for yourself and eat with the children, if your dietary requirements allow you to do so. Either way, you need lots of energy and stamina so managing your time to fit in a short break is necessary.

It is hard work and only you know your own limits and what you need to get through the day, so do take enough rest and prioritise your health and well-being. Don't get me wrong though, I am frequently snacking throughout the day; home comforts are one of the benefits of a childminding job role. Another benefit is the fact that you can eat home-cooked food at lunch, as opposed to takeaway like many commuters do.

Advice and ideas:

- If you're likely to forget, place sticky notes around the play area to give yourself reminders of affirmations and other forms of practicing self-care.

- Organise the areas used for childcare in a way that gives you easy access, to quickly grab the things you need and go.

- Cook meals in bulk and freeze them, so you can quickly heat them up later in the week.

- Make smoothies or juices to keep your energy levels up.

- Snack throughout the day on nuts, crackers and oat cakes (keeping spreads like humous in the fridge).

Books build writers

Reading is very important because it can also develop the ability to write well; it did for me, for sure. Childrens ability to read and write is heavily linked to language comprehension, which begins at birth. (Grenier 2023, 58–59). Language comprehension is developed through interactions with adults, such as an adult and child reading together, the adult speaking to the child about the world around them, as well as the use of songs, rhymes and poems (Grenier 2023). I remember reading poetry books which later influenced my ability to express my inner emotions through writing poetry. Having read my poems now as a grown woman, I am shocked by the literacy skills I had gained at such a young age. Words are powerful ways in which children can express themselves, whether through keeping a journal or diary, or

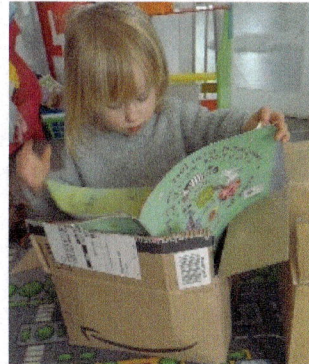

writing a story or book about something they love. Furthermore, the more diverse the range of books and language we expose them to the more literate they will become, gaining the tools to communicate effectively, in the way they choose to. This is why teaching children how to read in their early years of life, is extremely beneficial for their learning and development. They have the option of choosing books based on what they are interested in, as opposed to being read to, one of the ways in which they assist their own growth and learning.

If you have ever read the book You Choose (Goodhart 2018), you will understand the excitement that comes with being able to create your own scenarios, whether it's the kind of friends or family you would like, or simply what kind of hat you would like to wear. The style of the book allows the children to tell the story whilst exploring a range of different contexts: a great opportunity for children to learn about individuality and the right we all have to choose. Allowing them to explain their choices and encouraging discussion and comparison with their peers is something I love to do. The EYFS states children 'learn to make independent choices' and these adult-led interactions can lead them to being confident in doing that not just at story time, but throughout the day, every day. We want them to 'respond to new experiences that [we] bring to their attention (Department for Education 2021, 15). It is our job to help them understand how many different choices are presented in books: big hats with fruit on them, small ones that are called caps, hats made of straw, and the list goes on. Once we teach them the words used to describe each thing, we can talk about context and then link it with their real-life experiences. This can then lead to a conversation about similarities and differences which means children are learning from listening to others' experiences, rather than just focussing on their own choices.

Going back to literacy beginning at birth, I want to emphasise that everything children hear around them will form a piece of a comprehension puzzle. Dr Seuss says (Lord 2023, 4), 'The more that you read, the more that you'll know. The more you learn, the more places you'll go!' Children gain in depth knowledge of topics through exploring a diverse range of books; this knowledge can lead to success as they grow older. Through modelling correct pronunciation, expanding semantic understanding and repeating or rephrasing for clarity, we can begin a child's journey towards the attainment of literacy (Grenier and Vollans 2023, 61).

I love love love books and always remember when I was little my parents would take me to the library every Sunday; it was probably the most exciting day of my week. I make sure the children visit the library at least once a week. We don't just

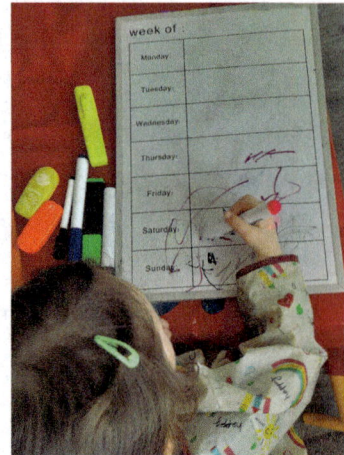

read the stories; we use actions, songs and different voices and expressions, asking and answering questions and counting along the way. Hearing a story from a disinterested adult reader, a child will likely display their own lack of engagement, so we must choose books we would read ourselves. As George Bernard Shaw says, it will show in the tone of our voice for sure (Lord 2016, 49). The same applies to setting up activities: they have to be interesting for the childminder, so you can teach it with enthusiasm, and in turn the children can maintain concentration.

Of course, to be quiet and still is not easy for toddlers, so sometimes they can only spend a short time reading independently. However, they always become quickly engrossed in books we read together. Nevertheless they need to be exposed to reading in a range of places, in order to differentiate between rules and boundaries in different contexts. You will find that they become better at being quiet and tidy across the board. The more I take them places, the more aware they become of the rules. Just as they tidy at home, they learn to take one book at a time and tidy it away before taking another out. Libraries (as well as children's centres and stay 'n' plays) also put special sessions on: story time, arts and crafts and song. We love attending and joining in as it allows the children to connect with group activities on a larger scale. I love that they have staff from the children centre's come in to lead each session, each bringing their unique personalities with them.

Reading can be wonderful outdoors as well as in: in a garden den, for example, or whilst laying on the lovely grass at the park. We take books on the train so we can read whilst travelling, as well as allowing children to take books home.

There is so much space for acting out stories and storytelling outside, inspired by or interacting with things we see in the moving, ever-changing world around us. In terms of literacy, you can help children to develop their gross motor skills by painting large letters on

tree stumps or using natural materials to form letters. Outdoor apparatus can easily be used as props and much more physical movement can be used in comparison with being inside.

One of the reasons I have preferred to buy books is because I have often found myself facing fines for overdue library books—that was before I realised using a child's membership card was the better option. I still buy books, however and I've learnt that they do not have to cost an arm and a leg. There's also always someone selling second-hand books in excellent condition, so I try to buy from local sellers. You have to be on the look-out and be part of groups in order to be informed of these book sales, or even just in touch with your local children's centre. Some just want to get rid of their unwanted goods as quickly as possible, so they do not mind giving them away for free. Whether bought or borrowed I teach the children to handle books with care, because you can only tape them so many times before they need recycling! Children learn from role models and from observing their environment; therefore, if the setting is full of torn displays and old books that are falling apart, they will most likely pick up similar habits. I feel it's very important to teach them a high standard of organisation and replenishment.

Advice and ideas:

- Build a den using a parachute, or any material you have in the house, along with large pegs and chairs, for a cosy space for reading time. Use projector torches and glow-in-the-dark shapes to create scenes. Pillows, blankets and (finger or hand) puppets can be used to act out the characters roles.

- Find car boot sales, market stalls and bookshop sales for bargain titles (note that the clearance section is not always easy to spot). Use voucher codes and cashback sites online for even cheaper resources.

- Ask family and friends or even clients for books they are getting rid of.

- Read rhyming words or sentences to children a few times to emphasise the patterns.

- Ask children what the rules of a group story time are before you begin, so that they can be fully respectful and considerate when others are talking.

- Act out stories, and spontaneously say lines you have read with the children in a range of contexts where links can be made.

House rules

Children learn to follow house rules through consistent and strict rule implementation. For example, the children understand that there is a process to setting up arts and crafts activities in order to avoid furniture or their clothes getting messy. Therefore, when I visit other settings and see that reading books have been scribbled in, it is clear to me that a room's set up has a huge link to a child's ability to follow rules. For example, the children that I mind have a clear understanding that they need to get the mat out first, then paper and then mark-making materials. They know they are not allowed to walk around with mark-making tools, and I explain to them why: this makes them more aware of how to look after their environment. The same rule applies to scissors, and any such tools stay on the table if the children decide to get up from their chairs. They are also aware that they must take responsibility for making a mess and help to tidy up, which they are very good at doing usually. The house rules stay the same from day one of their attendance, so they become familiar with them. An age-appropriate visual display is likely needed to ease their understanding, to remind them to implement routine into their daily lives.

When books are not handled with care it does make me sad, but they are treasured most of the time because of the repeated reminder to be looking after books. The children love them, and I have a strong connection to them from my childhood years. Nevertheless, making too many accessible will ultimately end with the children scattering them around the room and walking over them, so I encourage them to take one out at a time, as we do at the library. I recently visited a (fellow childcare practitioner's) house to buy some second-hand books and there were many that were in 'time-to-put-them-in-the-bin' condition. I am all for using tape to fix books but not too many times! Also, I do not think it looks presentable to have books that are scribbled in as part of the children's resources, nor will it represent a positive message about the setting's ethos. You need to teach children the consequences of breaking rules, for example, the ripping of books will result in them being taken away for repair or thrown away.

Taking into consideration all of the above, I have come to the conclusion that a playroom layout should reflect the house rules to some extent. For example, mark-making tools can be kept away from books, and scissors made inaccessible to the younger children (because they require close supervision). In this way, each area can be separated with an agenda in mind. I have worked at settings where they keep the new paperbacks out of reach only to leave the hardbacks out. This makes sense in protecting the easily torn paperbacks, however I have learnt this restriction is not always necessary. The fewer books that are accessible, the easier it is for us to manage them. Therefore, rotating books is a great idea. This method keeps children excited to read, linking them with the topics we are exploring together at any given time.

We do, however, keep library books separate so we can remember to return them and take extra care because they are not ours. It is a great joy to teach children how to be considerate of others' belongings, whether they are library books or the neighbours' front gardens.

In terms of indoor rules, I have learnt that children need to spend long periods of time outside—running, climbing, being loud—so that indoor rules such as 'only little voices' can work effectively. When I see children with surplus energy, I know I need to plan physically challenging activities such as parachute, tunnel, exercise or dancing time. They will usually stop when I reinforce what they should be doing rather than telling them off for what they should not. When they have not been out for long enough periods of time, I can always tell, because I see it in their energy levels: agitated and unable to focus. I love the fact that children require a balance of active and focussed play; this routine gives us childminders the opportunity to have the best of both worlds.

Advice and ideas:

- Be consistent and try not to give in when children are attempting to bend the rules, no matter how many buts or pleases you hear.

- Use methods like asking for 'hands in the air' when you want an organised discussion, or use repeated clapping patterns to get their attention if you want them to stop or be quiet. Save your voice!

- Put up displays of routines and rules where children can see them daily.

- Focus more on demonstrations and root causes of behaviour than immediate outcomes.

- Throw questions out to children and give them time to answer.

- Give them the responsibility of tidying, fixing or undoing what they have done so ignorance does not develop.

Back in my day

I sometimes plan activities I once did at school, such as tea bag painting. I love to teach children about history and information technology (as they called it in my school), simultaneously making links to EYFS development areas. I try not to underestimate the children's abilities and provide activities for them that are both challenging and not what they would do at home. Also, children have different ways of learning so adapting to individual learning styles is important. Sometimes being flexible, and extending your usual activities, is also necessary, to keep them stimulated for a longer period of time and to provide them with a deeper understanding of specific topics. As they say, children's minds are like sponges, so why not teach them first aid or dinosaur names? Children can, sometimes surprisingly, say bigger words if we give them the opportunity to.

I expose them to as much language as possible, readings signs and newspapers with them or to them. A language-rich environment can be the 'fuel that lights the fire,' according to Sandra Mathers, alongside the adult interactions that are the engine-room of language development (Grenier and Vollans 2023, 24). I agree completely with this theory and so value the planning that must go into organising a children's play area accordingly. We must help children to make links; consider where we place resources and each individual's interest areas. These will change with the children along their learning journey. Activities are much easier to plan if resources that can be easily linked are already together.

There is no point in putting books out that are too simple if you know the children coming in that day are very advanced in their communication and language; instead, try to focus on books they will never have heard of that discuss brand new concepts. I like to have books out for a week if the children are eager to read them repeatedly, then the following week I swap them over for new ones.

Correct pronunciation can take time, so children need us to repeat words back to them slowly in different contexts and whilst they are playing. Scaffolding (adding to the words children say) is necessary to bridge the gap between their current stage of communication, to the next. This technique also teaches them different ways of saying things; increasing their ability to provide detail in the form of descriptive language. Providing a diverse range of experiences will add to their home learning and cultural capital; many will never have done what they do with a childminder with their families. I frequently plan new places for them to visit, as it is important to teach them about diversity first hand; we visit everywhere from the zoo to the local places of worship. We talk about different lifestyles, what we see around us—like the graffiti of Hackney Wick—and learn about rules in context and road safety. Topics such as homeless people, race and poverty often spark questions and children are inevitably exposed to issues that are not pleasant to discuss. Nevertheless, they need to know

what is going on in the wider world, rather than just sitting comfortably in their innocent bubble. Is it not more beneficial to teach children about the real world rather than just preparing them for school? Being able to write their names and sit quietly to concentrate on focussed activities is important, but so is understanding how the world works: being able to explain where, why and how. The early years are the prime time to fill their minds with sprinkles of facts and knowledge.

It can become boring if you cycle through the same activities with those you're minding, which is why I try to think of exciting things I did when I was younger. Relatedly, I think it is important for childcare practitioners to plan activities they are interested in, so the children are on the receiving end of this energy and enthusiasm. Imagine going to a dance class and trying to learn from a teacher who has no expression and is in low spirits. I always find that no matter what is going on in my personal life, I am so much happier when I am working. They can sense when I am upset or not well and the empathy they show is extraordinary.

Advice and ideas:

- Use syllables together with clapping, or playing an instrument or music, to teach children how to pronounce big words.

- Old-fashioned activities are still educational and fun! You could try: tea bag painting, usings sticks to measure the depth of water, writing postcards, hopscotch, 'Hop, Skip, Jump'—for exploring different ways of moving and measurements, as well as space negotiation—games like 'Duck, Duck, Goose', board games or 'What's the Time Mr Wolf?'

- Ask parents what they do as a family at home and where they go: often they give me great ideas to try out.

- Go to exhibitions which are usually free, e.g., the Childcare & Education Expo, and network: speak to as many people as possible and pick up free magazines full of ideas.

- Magazines like Creative Steps, Childcare Professional and Nursery World, as well as Pinterest, are all fantastic sources for activity ideas.

YouTube is also good for visual demonstrations!

- Use loose parts and other abstract ways of encouraging children's creativity; everything does not need to be concrete or directly related. Think outside the box to make links.

- Don't be afraid to move the resources around and change the layout of a room completely; if it does not work, just change it again.

Positives first

Telling someone their positives alongside their negatives is more motivating than simply listing the latter. This feedback method is effective, whether it involves a manager and employee, or it's a conversation between friends. Growing up I learnt to be strong on my own because people would constantly put me down in an 'I'm right, you're wrong' kind of manner, like Matilda's father in the Roald Dahl classic; it made me want to be self-sufficient and fight for my freedom even more. I wanted to carry on being me, proud in my colourful personality that shone through naturally. Teaching children to be resilient but also confident in themselves, to stand on their own two feet and not let anyone take their self-esteem away, is essential for getting them through the struggles that life can bring. Hence why we must make sure they feel valued despite their weaknesses or mistakes; I teach them that we are all human and each have our imperfections. We can help children to overcome struggles by focussing on areas of the EYFS they may require support with: PSED for example (Department for Education 2021). By teaching one child to focus on their PSED, you will help them to spread a positive impact to others around them, setting a good example. Children who can demonstrate friendly behaviour, with an awareness of not just others' but their own feelings, are likely to motivate others to do the same. In light of this, we can give children tools to self-regulate if they are showing unacceptable behaviour.

The three prime areas (as in the EYFS 2021, 8) create a strong foundation that provides stability for the specific areas of learning, therefore, without them there will most likely be noticeable gaps in development that will form, such as a lack of social skills. This is why, for children aged three and under, childcare practitioners must solely focus on these prime areas. However difficult a child's behaviour is to manage we must always shine a light on what they are doing well. 'Choose your battles' is what I have been told in the past, meaning you cannot address everything at once, but you can prioritise instead. We all feel overwhelmed when someone gives us multiple things we need to work on simultaneously, and children are no different.

For unacceptable behaviour, there will be a few next steps you can mutually agree on with parents; these need to be the focus. Constantly having a go or reminding children of their mistakes will only bring down their self-esteem. They won't feel any motivation to do better. The more we criticise, the bigger the burden they have to carry with them day to day and into the future.

The effects of repeated negative comments can have a long-lasting impact on someone's mental health. Considering this, I have tried to give parents balanced feedback on a child when they arrive for pick-up: what has been going well but also the further support that is needed. Putting yourself in their shoes, you can understand that they may have already had a stressful day, hard at work, without having to hear their child has shown unacceptable behaviour. In addition, not all parents will appreciate feedback or updates whilst they are at work. Despite all the above, it is crucial to inform parents how the day is going, especially during settling-in periods. I see the

guilt on parents faces when they first drop off their child; they are anxious and reluctant to let go, so the reassurance we give them is most needed.

Each parent will have a different way of communicating and in turn expect a particular way of communicating from you. Once we have identified a family's individual preferences, we can learn the most effective communication. For example, some may prefer more details about daily activities, whereas others will want to know what the children learnt. Some will prefer a longer conversation at the door each morning or at pick-up, and in contrast others will drop and run, preferring to discuss their child via text. Some have a more serious attitude while others are much more laid back, taking most things light-heartedly.

When giving my assistant feedback I aim to tell them what is going well, then what they could improve on. Negative feedback alone may make them feel like their efforts have been flushed down the drain. I remember working in retail and being told that great customer feedback would show me how I should be working all the time, therefore it did not deserve any special recognition. On the other hand, when I made a mistake of any kind, I would be called to the manager's office immediately. I found this unfair, and my self-esteem was affected; I did not feel my hard work was appreciated. Constructive criticism is the most effective way to communicate feedback to your assistant, to support their continued professional development and for their mental health.

I would dislike an assistant to do everything in the same way I do, in a robotic sort of way, as children benefit from a team of diverse expertise, and therefore valuing individual traits is important in the workplace. This means understanding that we each have our own strengths and weaknesses, therefore partnership working (where each person contributes something of their own) should be used as an advantage. I once worked at a pre-school where one member of staff loved reading to the children, and another did not; partnership working is effective because each person's contribution is one integral piece of the whole puzzle. In terms of the registration process, you need to first find out about other settings the children go to and then collect information from the other professionals and adults in the child's life. This way you can exchange helpful ideas, new perspectives and expertise. Children are usually very different at home in contrast to the way they are at a childcare setting; I give them a structured routine and the children may see me as a teacher as opposed to a parent. They will be more comfortable at home because it is where they spend most of their time, so what we see as childminders is never the full picture.

It takes years to master the role of a childcare practitioner of any sort, including being a childminder, who works in a far more solitary way than most, so we must be patient with assistants and offer as much support as possible, addressing any concerns. There are many different learning styles in existence, and you need to work together with your assistant to find theirs. For example, you could use colourful charts, Post-it Notes, displayed reminders, books or magazines, and other ways of supplying them with important information and emphasising key words. There is so much terminology to remember that it can be overwhelming to learn all at once. Ofsted ask very specific questions, regarding safeguarding, for example, so using key words in particular can help us to be prepared in advance, rather than trying to cram lots in at short notice.

It is a learning curve, and assistants can learn through experience just as I did. The priorities are ensuring legalities are adhered to, such as safeguarding.

Advice and ideas:

- Always try to see the positives in everything (the silver lining never disappears) and make sure both children and assistants know how well they are doing.

- Be understanding of apprentices or newly appointed childcare workers who have very limited experience; put yourself in their shoes and be patient as well as supportive.

- We all start somewhere; by giving assistants' responsibility to do risk assessments, asking them to get the children's attention to make an announcement and praising them throughout the day, even if it's for things that seem small.

Flexible with limits

Childminders are running a business with policies in place and so cannot meet every single request that a parent makes. I have spent a long time being as thorough as possible when writing my policies; they are written in a way that covers both the child and their family and the childminder. It's understandable that we may sometimes need to further explain things, despite clear statements.

The importance of being transparent from the very first meeting and when issues arise is one of the biggest lessons I have learnt. I am open and honest on a daily basis, which means parents know exactly what to expect; when they do test us, we can use our policies as a shield! As long as they have signed to declare their understanding and agreement, they cannot argue against them, and thus they must either abide by them or terminate the contract. It is essential to thoroughly go through a contract whilst sitting with a parent, explaining it in detail, clarifying any points of concerns and answering questions with our full attention. If this is all discussed before the contract is signed, we are making sure the parent fully understands what they are signing up for, and therefore it is a mutual agreement (Lee 2014, 56). This process is highly effective in determining whether the relationship will cause stress or concern later. As Allison Lee discusses in her book How to be an Outstanding Childminder (Lee 2014), there are many points to consider in detail when signing a contract with parents; these include any changes to circumstances that means updates must be made, as well as having a review date in place, at which point we would check in with them in case they forget.

Increased flexibility is one of the qualities childminders bring to family life, and therefore assertiveness is a skill you need to manage your boundaries. Nonetheless it is a skill learnt over time; dealing with each family's individual requests is a lot of pressure. In being consistent in your approach you can ensure the needs of the business are being met, and you are not being too flexible whenever parents demand things of you.

Lots of childminders I know have made the mistake of not asking for a deposit at contract stage, of saying 'yes' too often or of offering services that do not fall within our specified job role. I once accepted lower weekly payments from a parent who came to me crying on a regular basis; it did not end well, and it turns out she did the same thing to another childminder previously. More respect can be gained by sticking to policies rather than by giving in constantly, which can show you undermine yourself. Taking myself seriously and having that self-respect is what has helped me build my self-esteem; you are not just letting children play under your supervision or working a 9–5 job that can be forgotten about as soon as the children have gone home. Being self-employed as a childminder means ongoing work and management responsibilities to maintain a high standard of business, let alone an 'outstanding' one. Taking this into consideration, I see that the joy lies in being in charge of what you do and when you do it, as well as how much you do. There is fulfilment to be found in the self-growth that occurs over the years, from being faced with difficult situations, handling families who complain and dealing with the consequences of mistakes we have made. This can all change a person over time for the better and will undoubtedly make you stronger!

Advice and ideas:

· Always take a deposit either before or on signing the contract.

· Stay loyal to your policies and never go against your business ethos.

· Go with your gut feeling and figure families out from the moment you meet them; do not ignore any red flags!

· When mistakes or conflicts happen, it is not the end of the world, and you are not a failure. This is just a small chapter of your life as a childcare practitioner and the person you become will be super proud for the 'keep-on-going' attitude you managed to dig out!

Do it now!

There have been so many missed opportunities for taking on new children at my business, due to not dealing with enquiries fast enough. Responding in a timely manner, as soon as I see the message ideally, works for me because I know I will otherwise get preoccupied with a million other things.

There are so many childcare options out there, which is why potential clients have already found something if I take too long to respond. Some parents will enquire just before their baby is born, or when they are still on maternity leave; not everyone is in a rush to find childcare, which is why taking a deposit is essential—a lot can change in the time between a booking and the intended start date. In light of this it seems reasonable that some childminders, considering the potential losses of a cancellation, will take the first week or month's fees to secure a child's place.

If they have not followed up after the first meeting, it is worth checking in for any updates. Not all parents will communicate efficiently, if at all, and this can be disappointing if I have spent my weekend showing them around my house and engaging them in lengthy, detailed discussions about childcare.

Being proactive in general is a skill needed for self-employment, and childminding in particular, to avoid the workload mounting up and making it seem like a long list of chores instead of a simple little assortment of things to do. This stresses me out and simple tasks become more complicated.

Advice and ideas:

- Focus on the priority tasks and goals; try not to endlessly write tasks under the heading of 'does not need immediate attention', and instead write up an action plan.

- Make communicating with families your absolute priority, especially when you are trying to grow your business. Clients do not just grow on trees: you have to do the work in finding them.

- Set aside a short amount of time to complete business-related tasks that need your attention, then enjoy your 'me time', and more than likely the hard work will pay off.

- Try to do a little every day, so that daunting tasks you have been pushing aside become simplified and therefore easy.

Let it go

When meeting with prospective clients I have learnt to be realistic as opposed to getting too excited initially; I remain composed throughout our meeting and consider the likelihood of them choosing another setting. I often come across parents who seem extremely keen during their visit and have even paid a deposit, but then they've disappeared. It is not the best feeling to find out what has actually happened through other sources, but it has made me realise this scenario is possible. I have learnt to let it go and move on, despite the horrible feelings that indirect communication can bring. I try to always end contracts on civil terms, however, sometimes it is not within our control. There is so much to learn from these experiences and resilience to be built. Dealing with yucky situations is a big part of running a business, hand in hand with the good.

Annoyingly, I regularly get contacted by parents whose first words are 'How much do you charge?', 'Are you available?' or 'I need childcare.' I do not appreciate messages of this sort: statements rather than enquiries, or one short question and no specific details. Advertising my business on a website as a professional childminder, I expect to be spoken to in a polite way with an introduction or greeting before a question, rather than the above. However, we must bear in mind that families each have their own ways of communicating, as well as not having much time, and are not sending out messages as professionals.

A detailed message means I can reply with availability based on their requirements, speeding up the process and avoiding an endless back-and-forth. One way of fast tracking the process is to ask for a contact number to speak over the phone. I like to ask questions about their child or children and get to know them a bit, to ensure our partnership can work. It is good to get a clear indication of a family's wants and needs, as well as their attitudes and personalities. Whenever this process takes too long, I have found they will just look elsewhere or that they've made assumptions about how busy I am.

Advice and ideas:

· Reply to messages as quickly as possible: you will appear to be on top of everything and they will most likely feel prioritised.

· Try to be decisive and straightforward about whether the requirements for both parties are a good match and only say yes if they are realistic and attainable.

· When an anxiety-ridden situation occurs, try to focus on what is going well and be patient with yourself throughout and afterwards. It is not easy to move on when dealing with something you care about.

Babysitting

Childminding is more than just looking after children and babysitting is more than just sitting in whilst the parents are out. I love babysitting because it gives me the opportunity to develop an even closer bond with the family. It is a lovely change for my childminding children, as usually they come to me to be looked after in my home. They get to show me around their house as well as their toys; how exciting, from a child's point of view! I have so much appreciation for families trusting me not only with their child but in their home whilst they are out! I have always found it interesting how people live and in particular how they decorate and organise their children's play areas. Babysitting is an opportunity to learn about a diverse range of lifestyles, therefore widening my own sense of inclusion.

I am also curious about how the child behaves at home, for me the task of observing children is not limited to my work hours. I am frequently making a mental note of their 'wow moments' (new things they are doing), or things that they need a bit more support on. Visiting a child's home is beneficial in many ways! Even if I stay a short time, it can make a huge difference to how well I know the family, therefore positively impacting on our relationship.

Building relationships with loyal clientele takes a long time and hard work; to keep them, even more so. I have known some of my babysitting families for several years, and consequently they have become like family. Seeing the children grow from babies to older children is the most rewarding aspect of childminding, and because I see them occasionally, changes are always easier to notice. It is incredible to know that the business has been grown from scratch, and, like a tree, the branches lead to many different clients. You must be prepared to reach them via advertising, whether through talking when out with the children or via online platforms. Another thing to note is because babysitting pays well it is worth doing weekends and evenings; however,

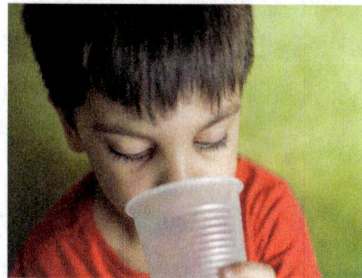

not everyone is happy to give up their valuable time to babysit. Having that flexibility to say 'no' is something that fits hand-in-hand with working during peak times, so I am not tied into any regular work.

In terms of the registration process for babysitting, there is less paperwork to complete in comparison with childminding, with policies already in place: only a contract is needed. The contract is simple, including emergency contact details and the child's personal information. A risk assessment is important and should include the location of the first aid box and keys. I remember one evening whilst babysitting, I heard a sound coming from upstairs, only to find there was a lodger staying over. Now I always ask if there is anyone else living in the property, to avoid this happening again. The same thing applies to pets or anyone who may be 'popping by'. Doing a home visit is beneficial in getting to know house rules and a routine in detail. The children may have milk before bed, for example, or require a bath.

When babysitting, I bear in mind that my childminding house rules are not the same as the family's rules at home, and even whilst out, I try and fit into their way of doing things. Getting permission to do something, if you're unsure that it's habitual for the child, for example, could be a cooperative move because parents are then making certain decisions. I enforce general childminding rules when babysitting, such as 'only little voices inside' and sitting down when eating. Regardless of their rules at home, I still encourage healthy eating along with a balance of active and more relaxing activities, and I remain strict on punctuality. I once babysat a child who asked for chocolate milk before bed, which, on checking with the parent, it turned out they were allowed to have, so I let them have it. However, on the second occasion they asked I just gave them warm milk for health reasons and the child was not fussed at all surprisingly. This goes to show that sometimes behaviours become routine and children, like practitioners, can follow these on autopilot. Unless we trial changes, we are not giving children the opportunity to break out of habits. I do not think we have any reason to feel guilty about challenging habits or set rules, as passing on our expertise can be beneficial to a child's future. There is no need to give children everything they ask for. I think it is good to build on their ability to adapt when things they want are not available; this encourages them to go without but also to find alternatives. Finding solutions to problems like this teaches children to be resilient.

I want families to use me again and to recommend me to others, so being professional is important to me; it also paves the way for maintaining a successful business. It really is joyful to build and keep relationships going. Sometimes, families do not check I have insurance in place or even certificates; most employ me through word of mouth, trusting their recommending source. Parents do not always know what to ask me, especially those who have never searched for a childminder before, in comparison with teachers or fellow professionals in the education sector.

'What if?' should always be a question parents keep in mind because unfortunately the worst could happen—that is the reality. It is totally up to individual childminders, when babysitting or otherwise, how professional they want to come across; the various levels will indicate how seriously the parents will take you. I feel I can justify charging more when I can show my portfolio of certificates and demonstrate in-depth knowledge. Also, I want them to see that I am a businesswoman who wants to be taken seriously. Nevertheless, parents may arrive to an appointment later than planned, perhaps losing track of time or experiencing delays of some sort, and expect flexibility from me. I do provide flexibility, which is why my services are very popular with parents; I do not mind if they are late, as long as they keep me updated so I know a rough time of arrival. If you are much stricter because you have set hours, make this absolutely clear from the initial meeting to ensure the hours you work are paid for. Babysitting really is similar to childminding in the sense that each individual family holds different values that you need to be aware of. If parents take advantage of the flexibility I offer and come late repeatedly, it would appear as though there's a lack of respect for my professionalism. To counter this, they need to be made aware that I will adhere to my policies for my own sake too.

Fortunately, the families who I babysit for currently have the most comfortable houses and they themselves are very accommodating and understanding. When you have been working all day, babysitting must be somewhere you can feel relaxed.

The babysitter can decide what they want and what they don't, so, for example, if I see anything to do with household chores in the job description, I do not apply. I clean and tidy around the child but not the house, generally speaking. I have in the past advised many families to search for a nanny or au pair if they require cleaning and childcare services or a 'mother's help'. They won't always know the difference between childcare roles so it is up to us to explain what exactly we can do.

Advice and ideas:

· Do only what you are comfortable with and don't be afraid to say 'no' to offers of babysitting hours.

· Try not to take on too much so you are being kind to yourself; health and well-being come first (easier said than done, I know).

- Be confident in what you offer and what you do not.

- Take someone with you, if you can, to an initial meeting at a new client's house to safeguard yourself.

- If you want, you can have a strict policy on lateness, whether it's in regards to payments or timings, and be consistent in following this through. If you feel it is necessary to charge by the minute during your unsociable hours, you totally have the right to!

- If something illegal or unjust is taking place in the client's home, seek help or advice; just because you are not in your own setting, doesn't mean you can't protect yourself and the child if needed, and particularly if legislation exists to support action.

- Signpost to parents if you do not want to keep explaining things; there are many websites that discuss topics such as the different types of childcare roles.

Attachments

When I leave the children with an assistant or back-up childminder, I feel what it must be like for a parent to leave their own children, especially when the kids only want me. It is the most heart-warming feeling to know you are needed and wanted; attachment is a beautiful aspect of working with a small group of children in a childminder's setting. It makes me more empathetic and able to understand the emotions parents must go through, perhaps feeling guilty despite how much they trust the carer. I too like to have updates that everything is going well even if I have only been away for a short time. When I return after my training to pick up the children at the children's centre creche, they come running to me and I feel so loved! I begin to imagine what the joys of parenting would be in these circumstances. When I am babysitting and they fall asleep in my arms because they are unwell, that too makes me want to have my own. I

feel so lucky to have such a rewarding job that makes me feel worthy and loved. For me, these aspects outweigh the hardships and struggles.

I find that making a child feel special not only boosts their self-esteem, but also allows them to feel closer to me. For example, a little party for a child's birthday or a graduation before they begin school; these experiences show children how much we care and how special they are to us. One of the joys to building close bonds with children in this way, is that they create positive memories with their special people, therefore giving them the reassurance they need for their future relationships.

Advice and ideas:

- Keeping in touch with past clients may not be for everyone, so only do it if you can realistically manage it with all the other demanding aspects of a child-minding role.

- Special books, home visits, selfies or photos of good times and 'wow moments': these all encourage attachments to form and to continue long term.

- Regular communication to see how a child you've looked after is doing, even if just once or twice a year, can be rewarding. You could send and receive updates and photos.

Apprentice vs qualified childcare practitioner

I feel so much more reassured and stress free when I have an assistant working with me; I have learnt the benefits and draw backs of hiring an apprentice versus a qualified practitioner. It is not easy letting a stranger into your home either way nor working with them so closely.

Training an apprentice is hard work, both in terms of paperwork and mentoring, as well as having an extra responsibility to role model. On the bright side, it is reassuring to have someone competent around to take charge; someone who can manage for a short time without me and who is able to take on all the responsibilities needed within the job role. Finding someone qualified has, however, proven very difficult for me, considering the shortage of qualified staff who are reliable and exhibit consistent communication. Bad first impressions of this kind do not motivate me to take their application to the next stage. Your considerations when hiring someone should prioritise how punctually they turn up to a trial day or interview, the quality of their interactions with the children and their attitude. Initially I feel it is better to wait to find employees who are a better match than to settle; it has to work for both parties.

Staff may seem eager and enthusiastic to learn when they begin working with you, which is extremely refreshing; however, keeping them on a long-term basis once trained can be a challenge. Nevertheless, there are lots of benefits to hiring staff: I feel so much more relaxed knowing I have back-up within my setting, for example, when I am sick or struggling with school pick-ups. With a childminding setting being managed by more than one person, it gives me peace of mind and takes the pressure off my shoulders. Other local childminders are generally very busy, so asking them for help is not always productive. They would prefer my minded child to attend their setting as opposed to them coming to mine, because they have other children to supervise. They may have a space available one week but not the next, so I try to find more flexible solutions. Being part of a childminder network and building a network of close friends who work in the childcare field is crucial for childminders to be able to keep a setting open consistently. Maintaining a strong relationship with these people long term is also a lifesaver!

In terms of staff who are not qualified, the benefit of training an apprentice is an opportunity for you to apply leadership skills and, considering the funding available, pay less for help. Costs are significantly reduced, especially if there's been an increase in the national minimum wage, as there has at the time of writing. In addition, you, as the employer, have a choice as to whether or not you keep the apprentice on. There are agencies that can find apprentices for you and offer support which (considering the hardship of searching) is very helpful! Many do not charge for this service, but take a cut of the apprentice's pay, another bonus for you, at least. I have been lucky enough to have had contacts in the childcare field for many years, working with people I know and trust. There are good and not so good factors in working with familiar people, one of the latter is being too comfortable in each other's presence. It is easier to disagree with someone you know, as opposed to your manager who has no personal relation to you. I have hired both qualified staff, and family and friends, as well as an apprentice. Over the years I have learnt that to maintain a healthy work relationship, personal and professional aspects must be separated. If procedures are in place, this can be easily done, but both parties need to be disciplined in following them. This means discussing personal issues outside of work, not letting conversations take priority over your interactions with the children and not letting legitimate concerns go because you feel obliged to. If you are prepared to take control of situations like the above, there is no reason why it cannot work. Many people advised me not to hire family or friends, however I have had positive experiences with this, and I understand the need to grab opportunities when they come along. People also said it would be a lot of work to take on an apprentice, but I am enjoying it very much! Being a role model for an apprentice is definitely a massive joy of childminding; it is extremely rewarding.

What if?

Thankfully I have never had to call for the emergency services, but as I am solely responsible for managing my childminding setting, strict procedures need to be in place just in case the unlikely should happen. Staying calm and acting in accordance with these procedures is much easier when the steps are practised regularly, for example during a fire drill with the children.

It is reassuring to see children applying their learning to their home environments, for example telling their parents to test the fire alarm. When we teach them life skills they can use them throughout their lives and use their experiences of learning in emergencies.

Placing important things such as the first aid kit,

daily register, front door keys (made inaccessible to children) and emergency contact details conveniently located, makes for a much quicker exit. Ensuring risk assessments are done throughout the day will no doubt result in hallways being clear of obstacles.

Having a responsible person (someone familiar to the children and able to step in during emergencies) is essential for childminders, whether working alone or with an assistant. This should be a person who is within reach and mine holds a relevant DBS (disclosure and barring service) certificate. There are bound to be times when staff are ill, or a trip to the hospital is needed, therefore back-up is needed. This allows us to focus on dealing with the actual emergency as opposed to searching for another adult to help with the children.

Another way of preparing children for emergency situations is practising first aid skills with them by suggesting various scenarios. For example, a trip to the fire station will certainly help them apply their knowledge to the real world. They become more confident in connecting their visual/sensory experiences with the protocols learnt within the setting.

Young children will pick up protocols and become more competent, the more frequently they are practised. When they begin using what they have been taught spontaneously in their play, you will know they are fascinated by the topic, and have taken it all in. Likewise for adults: the more we refresh our training and put our learning into action, the better prepared we will be.

Healthy hacks

Making healthy food choices is not a convenient matter; to overcome all the 'junk food' we are brainwashed with through external sources such as the media, strong willpower is needed. Firstly, habits need to be changed in order to gain a different mindset; we all have the ability to research healthy eating for ourselves via trusted sources. For me, my nutritionist has helped me to get where I am today, eliminating the processed, sugary and toxic foods I was consuming before. I remember the days when nurseries I worked at provided squash and sugary desserts such as rice pudding or flavoured yoghurt. There are so many alternative foods and recipe ideas for specific dietary requirements now and so much inspiration available for

healthy eating online. Many recipes in this modern world are simple, quick and easy, with only a few ingredients needed. Therefore, it is arguably easier than ever to avoid prioritising the cheapest or on-offer products, or covering food in sugar or salt. Instead you can use seasonings, like spices or herbs (paprika/garlic), or lemon, for example; children benefit from consuming a range of flavours in their food. I often give the children a slice of lemon with their pancakes; they love to squeeze the juice on independently. This provides them with an opportunity to develop fine motor skills as well as being able to decide how much they would like. We also allow children to cut up their own fruit using child-friendly knives, then add yoghurt; this is much healthier than a shop bought flavoured yoghurt that contains a high amount of sugar (as most do).

Many people prefer convenience foods because they live busy lives and lack the energy needed to cook complex meals, resulting in artificial ingredients within ready meals. I have always had a passion for nutrition, cooking and baking, along with keeping fit, so my nutritionist's advice has made complete sense to me. Despite the increase in alternative nutritious options in shops these days, it is not always easy to buy quality, healthy foods considering the financial cost of it all and the sacrifices one needs to make to afford it. Considering this drawback, I propose you simply make sure the ingredients are as colourful as possible: red peppers, purple beetroot, yellow sweetcorn, etc. This way they can consume their 'five a day' and a variety of nutrients along with it. There are so many simple recipes for making food from scratch like pizza bases made of yoghurt and flour. Healthy food recipes do not have to be expensive or complex; I myself do not like to stand up for too long cooking one meal!

Once you've set a goal, taking baby steps towards it will transform your life and may even inspire others to be healthier! It is difficult to be disciplined and change habits instantly, hence the importance of aiming to tick off one simple task at a time, such as clearing cupboards of unhealthy foods and replacing them with

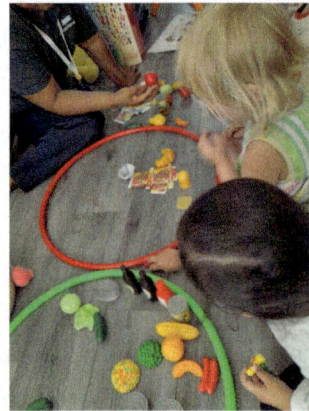

nutritious ones. Changes to health and well-being—in particular, energy levels—slowly come into noticeable effect. This is why it is important to persist with both patience and determination. In children I have noticed changes in their concentration levels as result of eating a nutritious and balanced diet; they are fuller for longer which impacts positively on their learning.

Growing up, when I would visit my nan's house, the junk food cupboard full or crisps, biscuits and cookies was my go-to when I wanted a snack. Robinsons squash was what I drank most of the time, impacting my teeth in a negative way. I now know first-hand that what you have in your home will be the foundation of your habits! The first thing I did when I began my new nutritional eating regime was to clear out anything artificial or unhealthy, tackling the cravings I had always had. These changes positively influenced everyone in my household; they were part of role modelling to the children I looked after.

Having a gluten-, dairy- and refined-sugar-free diet has opened my world up to cooking from scratch with plant-based ingredients only, therefore being fully in control of what goes into my body. When I started, I could not believe, and still cannot, how unaffordable plant-based food was, which is frustrating considering it should be more accessible to everyone. My nutritionist believes that instead of questioning why healthy food is so expensive, we should ask ourselves why unhealthy food is so cheap! When you walk into McDonalds and you see the 99p sign, how healthy do you expect it to be? Her outlook makes total sense and ties in with the way I now shop. Learning about nutrition and how to read ingredients has had a massive impact not only on my health, but on what I feed the children, as well as the depth of knowledge I can pass on. Children need to know why we are serving certain foods, how they can be beneficial and what effects they can have on their bodies.

I have always been careful about what I cook for children and how I cook it, but I now have more background knowledge and confidence to be able to teach them based on my experiences. Getting them involved means experimenting with a diverse range of recipes and allowing them to use their senses to explore. During the process they get to experience various textures, smells, shapes and colours. Breaking an egg, for example, is so much fun for a toddler, but requires skill to do it correctly. Younger children can learn where eggs come from whereas older children can take part in discussion about their vitamin D content. Children should be given opportunities to learn about a food activity or topic in a wider context than just what is in front of them; this means they can understand it better and not just hold onto one perspective. They may take time to try new things and alter their thinking to focus on what is good for them, as opposed to what just tastes good according to familiarity. Fussy eaters will often look at a dish and reject it instantly, but it is our job to role model being open to trying new things.

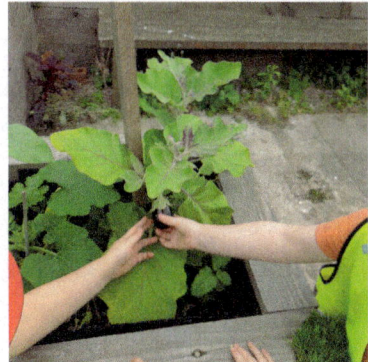

Cooking the same foods frequently can become boring so I tend to ask the children what they would like, giving them a few options to choose from. It is not realistic to expect children to like everything and eat everything; they must be encouraged to choose what they would like. The best we can do is to expose them to as many different foods and flavours as possible: the more food is offered to them, the greater the chance of them wanting it. In providing ingredients in a buffet style, you allow them to see and try as they please; my childminding children love a buffet.

I must say I thought it would be very time consuming to put all this effort into meal times, but it's not and it's definitely worth the extra attention to detail. Buying a different vegetable every week and finding new recipes to use it in is something the children and I love to do. For fussy eaters who pick out the vegetables they do not like, I try to compromise by telling them they can leave one out. Putting boundaries in place is just as important as giving choices as they need to learn how to maintain a healthy and balanced diet. Drinking water throughout the day, for example, is something they must do, even if just a few sips before and after their snacks and meals. By including these essential things in their routine, they will get into the habit of regularly drinking and keeping hydrated.

A sneaky thing I do is hide vegetables, for example, in pizzas under the cheese, though bear in mind that vegetables need to be cut into very tiny pieces for this to work! Kale, for example, is easily shredded, therefore it can be spread all over. In my experience children usually prefer smaller pieces rather than big chunks, otherwise they will pick bits out and eat the rest.

To avoid food wastage, I encourage children to take a little at a time and finish what they have before asking for more or leaving the table. If they still say, 'No more', telling them there is only a few bites left and counting with them makes it seem a little less work for them. Playing a game where you go away and then return to be surprised by the 'magic' of their food disappearing is another method that encourages children to finish their plate. Younger children may need feeding towards the end of their meal and suggesting they take a few more bites usually does the trick. A two-year-old who's with me currently frequently asks for more, takes a few bites, then says, 'No more', usually when others are finished and beginning to get up: she is distracted and not in the mood for eating anymore. I used to take excessive amounts onto my plate as a child, due to being very hungry, yet almost never finished it all. Children need to learn responsibility, in order to save food from being wasted, and get into the habit of taking a bit at a time. It takes time for them to learn portion sizes, but having a few rules for meal times is a big help.

Sometimes planning is needed before the cooking process and at other times a bit of 'bish bash bosh' does the trick; we made yummy muffins once when I created a recipe myself spontaneously! The fun is in the cooking process, when the children use their senses to explore. The worst that can happen is it doesn't taste great; however, learning is always present in these situations and that is positive. Most of the time, children see cake as yummy, even when you put a small quantity of sugar in or a sweet but healthy replacement. As long as there is no overpowering spicy or bitter taste, they do not refuse it.

One thing I have learnt about taste is that sometimes it's all in the mind; I once ordered macaroni cheese whilst out on a trip with the same two-year-old mentioned above, and only remembered after serving it that she no longer loved cheese. It made me laugh a bit as she sat there staring at it for ages (as though she had made up her mind before even trying it), so I explained to her that I did not add extra cheese to it. As soon as I said this, she had started eating and finished it all with no issues. I then realised she simply needed to know the content of cheese, and some reassurance to go with it. At my home she picks the cheese out, which is a new habit: she loved it a few months' ago. I am by no means encouraging lying to children, but I do think we can experiment with their dislikes to help them be willing to try before they form lasting judgements. This theory can be applied to many scenarios in life, such as a new activity or item of clothing: until they try, how will they know?

Generalisations

Children benefit from a diverse range of experiences, therefore, cultural capital should be a significant aspect of their everyday learning. One of my aims when childminding is to give them 'wow moments': when their faces light up and they become engrossed in what they see. Growing up I was lucky enough to have visited the theatre, a variety of restaurants and various famous landmarks; learn through hands-on activities, like swimming or bike riding; and regularly go on holiday to different countries. This cultural and active childhood influenced me to register myself for courses every summer that took my fancy, whether it was maths-related or Bollywood dancing or even calligraphy. I was eager to try something new with everything I did and had parents who would encourage me to do so. These experiences, no doubt, had a positive impact on my attitude towards and knowledge of the world. This comes across in my love for teaching children about the reality that surrounds us, and in how proactive I am in achieving goals and encouraging physical activity. For example, when I am teaching them about families, we talk about various lifestyles and how culture shapes the way we live. When they've asked for some lemon or seasonings in their food, and took an interest in smelling things, we've made a little box that has a range of herbs in it and their names. I want to teach them as much as possible about each topic we cover, because then they learn there is much more to something than what we see in its literal form. I want them to accept we are all different because of our various cultural backgrounds. We go to so many different places on our outings and celebrate diversity at our get-togethers with their families. We talk about our experiences together with our friends and exchange our thoughts. They learn that diversity is something to celebrate! When they question why someone is in a wheelchair, we discuss not only the possible reasons for them being in it, but what that means for us in terms of what we can be grateful for. I feel it is extremely important to talk about how we are all unable at times due to being ill, or injured; and in this light disability is in us all to some extent.

During a sign language class I'd enrolled in as an adult, I was taught that children need to learn the various uses of one object, and its subcategories and their uses. This is when I realised that generalising does not teach them specific uses or meanings of a single word, for example: there are many different types of brushes including paintbrushes, hair brushes, baking brushes and sweeping brushes. Children will only understand the differentiations between objects if we teach them specific properties rather than generalising: calling all types of 'brush' simply that, brushes over their uniqueness. One way of making children understand this is through repeating tasks that involve following instructions. For example, I will ask a child to get an apron and they must then focus on the context (what will we be doing with it?), because we have more than one kind of apron. Once they begin to make links like this and think about the different types of objects, as well as their different uses, they will be able to follow the instructions asked of them.

Here as one

The children often say things like, 'That's mine!', 'But I was using that!' and, contrastingly, 'You're my best friend.'

I have learnt that encouraging them to work together as a team, as opposed to competing, is their biggest lesson. Suggesting that children have a go together can guide them to think outside the box and prepares them to resolve problems independently of adults. I see them helping each other roll up the rug or carry something heavy together that one had been struggling with, and I feel immensely proud. They need to learn to work as a team and I believe that the best way to raise them to this level is not by running to their aid with a solution each time, but instead asking them what they think is possible. Asking the older or more advanced children to go

and help sets a positive example to those less able or younger. This method not only boosts one child's self-esteem and teaches responsibility, but it also demonstrates how to do things for each other. Repeated tasks like this can accelerate children's learning in all areas of development, compared to if they only rely on us adults. Teamwork like this strengthens relationships like no other interaction.

In relation to using the term 'friend/s', children can learn to include many fellow peers rather than saying, 'my best friend': we have lots of friends and not just one. This encourages them to accept others and build up tolerance and patience levels. Each child is unique and different, so it is crucial they learn to not just get on with everyone but treat many others as 'friends'. Therefore, each child will feel included as opposed to left out. I find that inclusion is not just a term to describe what childcare practitioners promote, but also an

important aspect children should carry out, too. Being excluded can have a negative effect on a child's self-esteem; result in attention seeking behaviour because they do not feel appreciated. Of course, there will be times when children want to play independently or just with one specific friend which is their choice, as long as they are open to bonding with everyone at the setting. Group activities and getting involved alongside introverted children can help them to gain friends, even if they prefer to play alone.

A highlight of working in a more intimate childcare setting such as a childminding one is that we play closely with one another and build a very close bond. Children also benefit from socialising with different children (as opposed to the one 'best friend') and I love to watch how the dynamics change depending on their personalities.

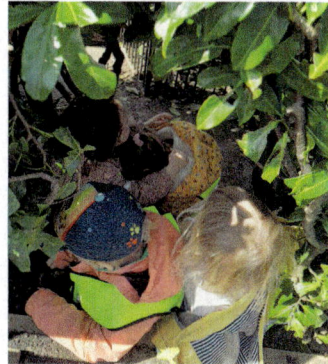

When you hear children use the word 'my' or 'mine' in reference to something they are playing with, think about how you can change this attitude to include everyone, as described above. Frequent reminders to say 'ours', for example, can influence a child's ability to see things using a more considerate approach and to develop their ability to share much more effectively. I have rules, such as, if you put something down, someone else can come along and use it, which help to set boundaries. These boundaries must be consistently used for every single child, for children to consider them fair and follow them.

All of the above will help children grow empathy towards one another, develop consideration and a 'we-can-do-it' attitude, rather than using 'I' all the time. The little things we do every day with the children are significant.

How to be 'outstanding'

To be an outstanding childminder there is no specific way of doing things or a template each childminder should be using; it is not a case of 'one size fits all'. I love visiting other early-years settings because I find it interesting to see the differences: what makes each one unique. Even though the Education Inspection Framework gives us information on exactly what Ofsted will be looking for, it does not tell us they need to see one way of teaching or a specific set-up. Their main concern is whether our teaching methods are effective, which links to how well we know our children.

It is our job to be aware of each child's cultural capital in relation to physical development, and provide opportunities that will help them to fill in any gaps. (Grenier and Vollans 2023, 47). For example, a child who does not have frequent opportunities to walk or take part in more challenging physical movement can benefit a great deal from learning to travel on foot. I have looked after children who were tired from one stretch of road, whereas some children are content to walk lots. These children are usually also excited to go on trains and buses and love walking whilst observing their surroundings. Taking a car everywhere not only takes away from the opportunity to experience the travelling process, but it also limits their physical development. Children learn to be patient (when waiting in a queue), that sometimes we have to stand (when there are no seats) and how to behave appropriately to suit a range of contexts. Some children will lack 'a wealth of previous physical experience,' and face inadequate support within their home environment. (Grenier and Vollans 2023, 47). These children can be encouraged to move freely and in different ways; they can be given a range of sports activities to do, including yoga, to improve their balance and coordination. Their negotiation of space can be developed whilst they travel and move through a range of different environments; they may need to sidestep to fit through a small space or walk quickly through the train station barriers, or they could have a go at walking along a balancing beam to challenge themselves.

Childminding is not what it used to be in terms of the paperwork involved; there are various governmental guidance documents that have been updated over the years, and which now focus much more on the teaching element of the job. Development Matters, for example, consists of 'everything we want children to experience, learn and be able to do'. (Department for Education 2021, 4). By referring to the Statutory framework for the early years foundation stage, you will find you can trust your professional judgment whilst using Development Matters as guidance only. In the first few pages of this document the utmost importance of our expertise is highlighted, which makes me feel empowered and therefore more confident in keeping up good practise. So why not take on the role of a childcare practitioner, or childminder? There are lots of informative documents for ease

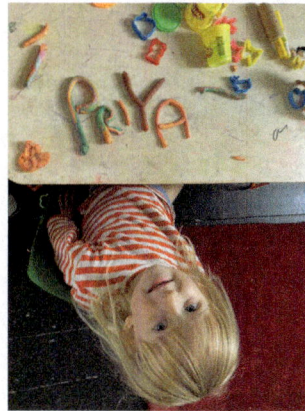

of reference and we can 'help children make progress without needing to record lots of next steps.' (Department for Education 2021, 4.) The number of different forms I kept years ago in comparison with now makes me stressed just thinking about it! There are helpful and in-depth explanatory notes included in the Development Matters document which really help you to understand better, for example, in chapter two: 'Seven key features of effective practice'. I find that the terminology is a lot more advanced and as a result makes me feel empowered to be using it in my everyday practise. 'No job is more important than working with children in the early years,' statements such as this shine a light on everything we do for the children in our care. (Department for Education 2021, 4).

Introverts and extroverts

Children should be happy in the choices they make, which is why free-flow play is important within a childcare setting. This means that whether they want to sit and read in a cosy corner of the playroom or go out to the garden and get messy, we must support them. When they are encouraged to take control of their play, they feel secure enough to be themselves. We can then identify their characteristics and learning styles, as well as interests, to keep them motivated to learn in the first place. Children's self-esteem is impacted in a positive way if we can identify and plan for their personalities, for example, by using the 'characteristics of effective learning' (how children learn) and schemas (repeated, or patterns of, behaviour). (Department for Education 2021, 13). So, for example, there is a child

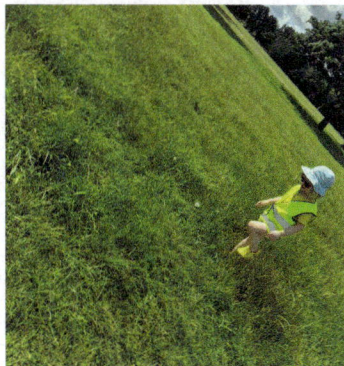

I look after who loves books and prefers to stay cosy inside for one-on-one time with me. Of course, it will not always be possible to stay in with a book as I am addressing multiple children's needs daily and often spend most of the day out, however I ensure she is made to feel valued and that her needs are met. Therefore we do also take books outside, and of course I encourage other types of outdoor time too, for fresh air, and with space to be physical—but where possible, in short spurts to suit her. Although the environment is changing, I make sure that she can still feel comfortable with her familiar resources close by. Other children will want to spend three hours in a row getting mucky and running around outside, which I also respect and make possible.

Focussing on the details of a child's personality is highly important in being able to provide for them; the loud and assertive children learn how to be considerate, for example, to not interrupt others when they are speaking. Quieter children who take longer to say sentences are given the time to speak, but also opportunities to be brave and speak up, for example, asking a member of staff for some water at a café. Learning styles vary and we can adapt our teaching to suit individual needs. In the article 'Nurturing their Potential' (Baker 2023, 42–43), to which I contributed, the theme of supporting advanced children is explored, with lots of tips, including allowing children to focus on their choice of play. Some ideas include using loose parts, an hourglass and big dice, however, these are not just going to help advanced children to learn but be beneficial to all stages of development. They can be called inclusive resources because there is something for everyone to learn or benefit from, in different ways. Another thing that is important to consider is what happens when the extrovert–introvert personalities collaborate or clash: they are learning from each other. Being role models for each other, learning from someone completely different and being able to adapt their usual ways of thinking: these are all learning moments for children.

I do not agree in making everyone do the

same activity and we have to consider that children will never be good at everything, for no-one is perfect; they will excel in their own time and within different areas of learning to one another. So, it is just as important for us to give our attention to introverts as it is to extroverts, being flexible in our approach and having a high standard for every single child regardless of personality traits.

As tricky as it may seem, it can be done by ensuring everyone's voices are heard and valued, to ensure one personality is not overpowering another. Teach them to be patient when listening, to use phrases like 'I think' and to acknowledge that everyone has a different point of view. Asking children questions whilst reading to them is a great way to not only encourage verbal participation, but also to show them that their opinions matter.

We have the fantastic job of watching children grow in their own unique ways, as whether loud or quiet, fast or slow: they are learning.

Advice and ideas:

· Choose resources carefully and consider the introvert–extrovert spectrum across a range of age groups rather than choosing specifically for the age the children are currently.

· You could select things like beanbags (for throwing and catching), pillows or blankets, a tunnel, a parachute game (with large clips for easy handling/ for clipping onto furniture) and soft toys.

· Ensure children, whether shy or boisterous, have daily opportunities to take responsibility and to speak up if they need something, rather than doing everything for them.

· Creative all-inclusive playrooms with books of all kinds, balls of different sizes, props and dress-up costumes with accessories such as masks and sunglasses.

· Offer children interactive/critical thinking resources such as a clock, a weather board or number games such as a children's dart board.

- Leave a whiteboard out and give children markers if they express the desire to write.

- Little lego and small world toys/signs/working traffic lights for children to create using their imagination and use representations.

Afterword

Considering the many benefits of a childminding role, I hope to be in it long term. These include uncapped earning potential, networking with other professionals, ongoing CPD opportunities and the flexibility of downsizing or expanding if you choose. If you are willing to put in your time and effort to help children and their families then this job is for you, although remember: you are the one who must set your boundaries. What works for one person will not work for others: the business needs as well as your personal circumstances should be kept in mind when starting out. I am currently able to have a more than comfortable lifestyle whilst gaining the other non-monetary benefits of the hard work I put in, which is perfect for me. As a business owner who started out young, I highly recommend going for it (whether it's childminding related or not) and do not stop until you get to where you want to be. Now at nine years old, my business makes me extremely proud; I see how much I have developed, and I hope to pass on all my expertise to others.

Glossary

Characteristics of effective learning: How children learn through developing positive attitudes and abilities.

CPD: Continuing Professional Development, the development of skills and knowledge that are needed for a professional job role.

Cultural capital: celebrating the diversity and cultural difference children bring into a setting, and providing experiences that they have not yet had the opportunity to.

EYFS: the Early Years Foundation Stage consists of a statutory framework that Ofsted use to inspect early years providers, and the non-statutory framework which offers guidance in relation to the learning and development of children aged 0-5 years.

Observations: A factual statement that is made by closely monitoring a child. Narrative observations may be longer when they are involved in a focussed activity.

Ofsted: Office for Standards in Education, a government organisation who are responsible for inspecting and regulating schools and childcare settings, as well as educational services.

Policies: A setting's individual standards that all staff and parents/carers must abide by, which are regularly reviewed (usually every 6 months or annually).

PSED: Personal, Social and Emotional development, a prime area in the EYFS.

Risk assessment: Identifying hazards that may cause harm, putting measures into place to manage them and monitoring outcomes.

Responsible person: An adult who is known/familiar to the children in a setting and able to take care of them in emergency situations.

Scaffolding: Building on a child's current stage of learning and development by interacting with them (at specific moments), in order to extend their knowledge.

Schemas: Repeated patterns of behaviour that help us to identify children's interests and preferred ways of playing.

SENCO: Special Educational Needs Coordinator, the point of contact for concerns when a child needs extra support in their learning.

Transition: Life changes that occur throughout a child's early years, that will affect their learning and development.

Bibliography

Department for Education, 'Development Matters: Non-statutory Curriculum Guidance for the Early Years Foundation Stage', Gov.uk, last revised July 2021, https://assets.publishing.service.gov.uk/government/uploads/system/uploads/attachment_data/file/1007446/6.7534_DfE_Development_Matters_Report_and_illustrations_web__2_.pdf.

Department for Education, 'Statutory framework for the early years foundation stage.' Gov.uk, last revised March 2014,

Statutory framework for the early years foundation stage (publishing.service.gov.uk).

Goodhart, Pippa, *You Choose* (London: Penguin Random House, 2018).

Grenier, Julian, *Succ essful Early Years Ofsted Inspections: Thriving Children, Confident Staff* (London: Sage, 2017).

Grenier, Julian and Caroline Vollans, *Putting the EYFS Curriculum into Practise* (London: Sage, 2023).

Lee, Allison, *How to Be an Outstanding Childminder*, 2nd ed. (London: Bloomsbury Education, 2014).

Lord, Kathryn, *There's More to Books than Reading: How to Help Your Child Bring Stories to Life* (Poland: CreateSpace Independent Publishing Platform, 2016).

Manners, Lala, 'Physical Development', in *Putting the EYFS Curriculum into Practice,* eds. Julian Grenier and Caroline Vollans, 44–57 (London: Sage, 2023).

Ofsted, 'Early Years Inspection Handbook for Ofsted-registered Provision', Gov. uk, last updated 14th April 2023, https://www.gov.uk/government/publications/early-years-inspection-handbook-eif/early-years-inspection-handbook-for-ofsted-registered-provision-for-september-2022.

Ofsted, 'Education Inspection Framework', Gov.uk, last updated 14th July 2023, https://www.gov.uk/government/publications/education-inspection-framework/education-inspection-framework#what-inspectors-will-consider-when-making-judgements.

PACEY, 'Bright Ideas', *Childcare Professional*, Autumn/Winter 2021.

Peacock, Alison, 'Afterword', in *Putting the EYFS Curriculum into Practice*, eds. Julian Grenier and Caroline Vollans, 192–193 (London: Sage, 2023).

Ratcliff, Wendy, 'What do I need to do to prepare for my early years inspection?', *Ofsted: Early Years (blog)*, Gov.uk, 25th January 2023, https://earlyyears.blog.gov.uk/2023/01/25/what-do-i-need-to-do-to-prepare-for-my-early-years-inspection/.

Tassoni, Penny, 'Sounding It Out', Childcare Professional, Autumn/Winter 2021.

Despite the challenges that childcare practitioners have faced in the recent years there is much to celebrate, as explored in this book. Written for the newbies, oldies, wannabes and flourishing childcare practitioners out there, this book has been written to inspire, empower and enlighten.

Childcare expert Priya Kanabar offers readers plenty of useful tips, as well as bright ideas to overcome the daily struggles we face. Everything from starting up a home-based childminding business, to maintaining a successful and joyous one for many years to come.

Printed in Great Britain
by Amazon